ITIONS

MENIAN
LGARIAN
RMESE (Myanmar)
INESE (2)
NISH
ITCH
GLISH
Africa
Australia (2)
Chinese/English (2)
India
Indonesia
Korean/English (2)
Korean/English/
Japanese
Myanmar
Philippines
Singapore
Sri Lanka
United Kingdom
United States (6)
TONIAN (3)
ENCH (3)
EEK
JARATI
NDI
NGARIAN (2)
N/ENGLISH
OKANO
DONESIAN (2)
LIAN
PANESE (2)
NNADA/ENGLISH
WAHILI (2)
REAN
KI
LAYALAM
ITEI
RWEGIAN
IYA
LISH (2)
RTUGUESE
rica
azil (3)
rtugal
SSIAN
HALA
NISH
ribbean
xico (2)
uth America
ited States (2)
DISH
L
IGU
(2)
J
HEI

(radio)

YOUR PLACE TO MEET GOD

Sarah Wilke
Publisher

Lynne M. Deming
World Editor

INTERDENOMINATIONAL
INTERNATIONAL
INTERRACIAL

79 EDITIONS
38 LANGUAGES

The Upper Room
May–August 2012
Edited by Susan Hibbins

The Bible Reading Fellowship
15 The Chambers, Vineyard, Abingdon OX14 3FE
Tel: 01865 319700; Fax: 01865 319701
Email: enquiries@brf.org.uk
Website: www.brf.org.uk
BRF is a Registered Charity

ISBN 978 1 84101 845 4

Acknowledgments

Printed in the UK by HSW Print.

The Upper Room: how to use this book

The Upper Room is ideal in helping us spend a quiet time with God each day. Each daily entry is based on a passage of scripture, and is followed by a meditation and prayer. Each person who contributes a meditation to the magazine seeks to relate their experience of God in a way that will help those who use *The Upper Room* every day.

Here are some guidelines to help you make best use of *The Upper Room*:

1. Read the passage of Scripture. It is a good idea to read it more than once, in order to have a fuller understanding of what it is about and what you can learn from it.
2. Read the meditation. How does it relate to your own experience? Can you identify with what the writer has outlined from their own experience or understanding?
3. Pray the written prayer. Think about how you can use it to relate to people you know, or situations that need your prayers today.
4. Think about the contributor who has written the meditation. Some *Upper Room* users include this person in their prayers for the day.
5. Meditate on the 'Thought for the Day', the 'Link2Life' and the 'Prayer Focus', perhaps using them again as the focus for prayer or direction for action.

Why is it important to have a daily quiet time? Many people will agree that it is the best way of keeping in touch every day with the God who sustains us, and who sends us out to do his will and show his love to the people we encounter each day. Meeting with God in this way reassures us of his presence with us, helps us to discern his will for us and makes us part of his worldwide family of Christian people through our prayers.

I hope that you will be encouraged as you use the magazine regularly as part of your daily devotions, and that God will richly bless you as you read his word and seek to learn more about him.

Susan Hibbins
UK Editor

In Times of/For Help with . . .

Below is a list of entries in this copy of *The Upper Room* relating to situations or emotions with which we may need help:

Acceptance: July 3, 4, 17, 27; Aug 2, 16
Anger: May 1; July 7, 31; Aug 28
Anxiety: May 3; June 17, 30; July 21, 26, 29; Aug 15, 20
Bible reading: May 4, 21; June 5, 10, 27; July 2, 20; Aug 10, 26
Change: June 10, 12, 25; July 16, 26
Christian community: June 5, 7, 23, 30; July 6, 11, 20; Aug 1, 11, 23
Creation/nature: May 5; June 3, 6; July 12, 15; Aug 6, 9, 30
Death/grief: May 4, 17, 28; June 2, 17, 28; July 19, 22, 28; Aug 19
Doubt: July 11
Encouragement: July 13, 15, 26; Aug 20
Evangelism: Aug 11
Failure: May 2, 23; June 1, 4, 14; July 12, 30; Aug 18, 23
Family: July 11, 18, 20, 21, 27; Aug 2
Fear: May 9, 16, 28; July 11, 23; Aug 23
Financial concerns: July 16, 28
Forgiveness: May 1, 30, 31; June 7, 24; July 7, 23; Aug 14, 27, 28
Friendship: July 18, 20, 23; Aug 4, 11, 16, 20, 23
Generosity/giving: May 5, 31; June 16, 20; July 1, 9; Aug 31
God's love: May 2, 4, 31; June 2, 4, 24, 26; July 3, 8, 30; Aug 16, 21, 31
God's presence: May 1, 22; June 9, 10, 17, 19; July 8, 10, 15; Aug 4, 25
God's provision: July 6, 16, 27, 28
Gratitude: May 10; June 22; Aug 8, 12
Growth: May 14, 15, 24; June 25; July 12, 24; Aug 9, 15, 23
Guidance: May 18, 22; June 3, 23; July 5, 11; Aug 3, 6, 26
Guilt: May 30; July 13
Healing/Illness: May 7, 10, 21; June 5, 15; July 6; Aug 5, 7, 19
Hope: May 7; June 4, 6; July 12, 16; Aug 5
Hospitality: May 16; July 4
Job concerns: July 7, 16; Aug 5, 19
Living our faith: May 2, 11, 31; June 5, 28, 29; July 9, 19; Aug 1, 3, 31
Loss: May 4, 7, 28; June 2, 15, 17; July 6, 30; Aug 5, 19
Materialism: July 3, 14; Aug 16, 29
Mission/outreach: May 11, 26; June 6; July 1, 4, 20; Aug 30
New beginnings: July 7
Obedience: May 3, 9, 27; June 11, 29; July 9, 13, 29; Aug 13, 27, 31
Parenting: May 2, 8, 30; June 4, 8, 22; July 2, 14, 21; Aug 10, 26
Patience/impatience: June 1, 3, 4, 9
Peace/unrest: May 7, 21, 28; June 13; July 8; Aug 25
Prayer: May 13, 27; June 6, 13, 27; July 5, 6, 25; Aug 1, 7, 28
Priorities: June 8, 12, 18
Salvation: May 12, 29; June 7, 12, 22; July 19; Aug 12, 17, 27
Serving: May 6, 19; June 1, 20, 29
Sin: May 2, 14, 14, 29
Speaking about faith: May 8; July 19, 31; Aug 1, 3
Social issues: May 9, 16, 28; June 15, 25; July 4, 6, 20; Aug 22, 30
Spiritual practices: May 4, 18, 24, 29; June 5, 13, 18, 23
Stewardship: June 8; July 1, 9
Temptation: May 2
Tolerance: May 16; July 4; Aug 30
Trust: May 3, 5, 28; June 11, 15, 27; July 16, 21, 29; Aug 15, 20, 25

Enabled by the Spirit

Acts 2:1–8

When we read the Pentecost story, we're struck by its power, but also by its mystery: the winds, the tongues of fire, the multitude of languages. How could they all be understood?

Last year, we began gathering our Upper Room ministry staff and volunteer editors around the globe into regional 'family reunions'. The first event, in Sao Paolo, Brazil, drew together our Upper Room and Emmaus/Chrysalis leadership from the Caribbean and Latin America. For four days, 32 of us assembled in a retreat centre for fellowship, learning, sharing and worship in English, Spanish and Portuguese.

At times we had translators, but primarily we relied on our own limited second-language skills and hand gestures to help us communicate with one another. It was exhausting and exhilarating. Even under these limitations, the work was moving forward.

The greatest gift of our time together came after closing worship and Holy Communion. We sang the final hymn, and we heard the benediction. Then someone began to quietly hum, reprising the final hymn. Softly, another began to sing the words in his native language, then another and another, then all. Though the words on our lips were in Spanish, Portuguese and English, we sang with one voice, and we could feel the fire of Pentecost move through the chapel. Neither culture, nor nationality, nor even our foreign tongues could separate us.

The crowd that witnessed the flames of Pentecost asked: 'How is it that we hear, each of us, in our own native language?' (Acts 2:8, NRSV). The answer then was the same as it is today. The Holy Spirit has the power to unite us in one voice as we carry the singular message of Christ's salvation into the world.

Sarah Wilke, Publisher

'Oh, no!' I cried, as I tried in vain to stop my favourite coffee mug from falling from my hand during the washing up. Our kitchen floor is hard and unforgiving, and seconds later my mug was smashed into countless pieces.

Faintly ridiculous though it is to get upset about a broken mug, I felt sad. I had first bought that mug when I was at university, simply because I liked the shape, and it had been with me through graduation, my first job, when I got married, surviving a number of moves and packing and unpacking numerous times. It was familiar to me.

We unearthed a beautiful mug from the cupboard that had scarcely been used, and which I am ashamed to say I had never really looked closely at before. We had had it some time, but rather than using it I had stuck with my old faithful instead.

Musing on mugs (I know, I need to get out more) I wondered if I am the same about aspects of my faith. Do I stick with the familiar routine I am happy with, attending the same types of church service, mixing with the people who have roughly the same beliefs as I do, reading the same kinds of books and articles as I usually do?

What if I am missing out by not trying new forms of worship? What if God is waiting to bless me through meeting new people with radically different views from mine? And as for reading, there are hundreds of writers who might have something new to say to me about my faith, even if it does not make comfortable reading.

Sticking with the familiar might be more appealing, but God has other ideas he longs to share with us: 'See,' he says, 'I am making all things new' (Revelation 21:5). Life lived in God will always include unexpected blessings of grace.

Susan Hibbins
Editor of the UK edition

Bullied

Read Psalm 35:17–28

O Lord, you have seen this; be not silent. Do not be far from me, O Lord.
Psalm 35:22 (NIV)

Throughout my school days, I was constantly bullied and teased. I learned to live with it, but many times I came home in tears, wondering why God was doing this to me. When my class's ten-year reunion was announced, bitterness and anger filled me as I recalled what some of these people had done to me in the past. I sought solace in the word of God. I stumbled upon Psalm 35 and was floored. God spoke directly to my heart through the psalmist's words about not letting enemies laugh at him or hate him when they have no reason.

This psalm explained so clearly my current feelings about my past bullying experiences that my anger dissipated in seconds. I realised that God was fully aware of how I felt, had always been aware of the pain that the bullying caused, had not wanted it and had never abandoned me during those difficult times.

Bullying is always damaging and painful for those who endure it, no matter how we try to explain it. But that doesn't mean that the victims of bullying have to live with pain, anger and bitterness for ever. God is always with us in our times of trial, and wants to free us from preoccupation with past hurts.

Prayer: *Dear God our Helper, remind us often that you are with us no matter what we face and that your word holds the answers to how we can respond. Amen*

Thought for the day: God can free us from our anger over past hurts.

Justin Swartz (Pennsylvania, US)

`RAYER FOCUS: THOSE WHO ARE BULLIED

Wandering Ways

Read Proverbs 4:25–27

My child, give me your heart, and let your eyes observe my ways.
Proverbs 23:26 (NRSV)

The bewildered child stood alone on the street in front of my house. I was alarmed, especially since none of my immediate neighbours has young children. He was not afraid as I approached him, and he willingly took hold of my hand. We chatted as we walked down the street toward a home a couple of streets away, where I knew a family with young children lived.

He told me that his name was Heath and said, 'I love ants.' Apparently, his interest in ants had lured him from the security of his own garden. He had followed the tiny insects until he ended up in a place he didn't recognise.

We're all a bit like that child. We may not deliberately take a wrong path, but the enticements and busyness of life can distract us and cause us to wander from close fellowship with God. Sometimes we end up in unpleasant or even dangerous circumstances we wish we had avoided.

God longs for us to return from our wandering. Just as Heath's mother rejoiced when she saw us walking toward their home, God is delighted to send love and forgiveness to wash over us when we head toward home.

Prayer: *Dear Lord, forgive us for not giving relationship with you priority in our lives. When we wander, draw us back to you. Amen*

Thought for the day: While we wander, God waits in love.

Muriel DeLong (New Brunswick, Canada)

God is for Us!

Read Philippians 4:4–9

If God is for us, who can be against us?

Romans 8:31 (NIV)

Earthly kings and leaders come and go. Some are good. Some do much damage before being voted out or deposed. In the USA, we have the chance to change our leader every four years. But the King of glory is one we can depend on eternally.

I remembered this recently when a distraught friend complained about events in the news. To him, the world was headed for destruction.

'If we both die tonight, what does it all matter?' I responded. 'All God will ask us about is our actions in life, the things we had choices about.'

He gave me an astonished look. 'I never thought of it like that. I suppose we have to leave a lot of things to God.'

We can sicken ourselves with worry over things beyond our control. Of course we do what we can to respond to the world's serious problems. Granted, we are concerned about politics, the weather, the economy and a host of other things. But beneath all this, God is a good God. When we reflect on this fact, contemporary events cannot separate us from the joy that comes from having a loving Saviour who is always at work for good—regardless of what the news is.

Prayer: *Dear God, help us to remember always that you are King of kings and that you take care of us. Amen*

Thought for the day: When we believe in God, we can see goodness in life.

James E. Bell (Missouri, US)

Love Letters

Read 1 John 4:7–16

God so loved the world, that he gave his only begotten Son, that whosoever believeth in him should not perish, but have everlasting life.
John 3:16 (KJV)

My husband died nine years ago. Recently, I came across the letters he wrote to me while we were dating almost 60 years ago. When I saw the familiar, hard-to-read handwriting, I smiled, remembering the excitement I had felt when a letter from him arrived. As I read the letters, I felt again the joy of knowing that he loved me. Through the years of our marriage, he demonstrated his love in many ways. I thank God for blessing me with a good man's love.

The Bible contains love letters from God—not romantic love, of course, but love that is deep, powerful and steady. Throughout the scriptures, we read of God's love and mercy, first to the Hebrew people, in providing for their physical needs and spiritual development. God's greatest love comes to us through Jesus Christ. In Jesus' life, teachings, death and resurrection, the love of God becomes real and we know that we are loved deeply and completely. We can be filled with joy as we praise God and give thanks for God's unending love.

My husband's letters went back into the box to be stored away. But my Bible is close at hand so that as I read it each day, I receive assurance of God's love.

Prayer: *Thank you, Lord, for your love letters in the Bible, and for your gracious love shown in Jesus, our Saviour. Amen*

Thought for the day: Look for ways God shows love for you and find a way to show God's love to those near you.

Joan S. Hutcheson (Georgia, US)

Feed the Birds

Read Matthew 6:25–34

Strive first for the kingdom of God and his righteousness, and all these things will be given to you as well.

Matthew 6:33 (NRSV)

Every morning, regardless of the weather outside, a variety of birds comes and waits for us to throw breadcrumbs out on the lawn. All sorts of birds come—the plain little sparrow, finches, blackbirds and many doves and pigeons. These birds know that we will give them food, and as soon as we go inside they fly down and enjoy the feast.

Our Creator is abundantly more generous than we are. Jesus told us not to worry about food and clothing; God will feed us and will clothe us more beautifully than the lilies of the fields.

During a rather difficult period some time ago, I worried terribly about how we would cope financially—until I read the Matthew 6 passage more closely. Yes, I of little faith! How many times did I need God to remind me that what we need will be provided? Through faith, prayer and growing trust, I turned to God and focused on what was important—to obey and do God's will. My burden of fear was lifted, and God provided for us in abundance.

Prayer: *God of all compassion, help us to see your hand at work in our lives. Teach us to trust your love and provision from day to day. In Jesus' name we pray. Amen*

Thought for the day: How is God providing for you physically, spiritually and emotionally?

Renny Stoltz (Gauteng, South Africa)

The Power of Humility

Read John 13:1–20

Jesus, knowing that the Father had given all things into his hands, and that he had come from God and was going to God, got up from the table, took off his outer robe, and tied a towel around himself.
John 13:3–4 (NRSV)

The description of the Last Supper can move us deeply. Yet beyond the ritual of foot washing, something tremendous is being revealed in these verses. This story of Jesus washing the disciples' feet declares the values of God's kingdom by placing them against the values of this world. The truth in these verses has the power to change the world.

We are assured that Jesus had received 'all things into his hands' because God had placed them there. As a result of this power, Jesus, knowing that he possesses power, gets up from the table and assumes the role of a servant. This is the connection the Gospel of John makes: because of Jesus' power, he washed the disciples' feet.

We live in a world where might is worshipped and weakness is despised. As proof of this, look at how much money many nations spend on weapons of war. To this world Jesus comes and says, 'In God's kingdom, this is what the powerful do: they serve the weak by becoming servants.' Jesus calls us to use our power in order to serve.

Prayer: *Dear Lord Jesus, help us to see you in our weakness. Help us to love and serve others. In your name we pray. Amen*

Thought for the day: We show God's power when we choose to serve the weak.

Link2Life: *For a link to a list of nations in armed conflict, go to www.upperroom.org.*

Katerina Katsarka Whitley (North Carolina, US)

Deferred Hope?

Read Psalm 146:5–10

Hope deferred makes the heart sick, but a longing fulfilled is a tree of life.
Proverbs 13:12 (NIV)

My heart should have been racing with anticipation, but instead I had been consumed by anxiety as I sat awaiting a scan. Fear had filled me during this second pregnancy. Just nine months earlier, a scan had shown that the 13-week-old foetus in my first pregnancy had no heartbeat.

My husband and I are Christians, but our earlier loss reinforced the truth that faith does not guarantee a desired outcome. We hadn't been able to bring ourselves to buy what we'd need for the baby, discuss names or even tell people we were expecting. When this scan showed the heartbeat of our second foetus to be strong, we expected to feel relief. Instead it somehow made us feel we had even more to lose. Eventually I gave birth to a healthy baby boy, but I missed out on the joy of pregnancy and on the peace that only God can provide.

The problem with deferring hope until a situation stabilises is that many situations never will. Hope in anything except God makes our hope depend on circumstances. But basing our hope in God means we can find joy in situations where joy should not exist.

Prayer: *Dear heavenly Father, teach us to hope regardless of our situation. May our hope be contagious, and may we always remember that true hope is found only in you. Amen*

Thought for the day: Christian hope is based in God, not in circumstances or emotions.

Kristen Escovedo (Texas, US)

Perspective

Read Romans 8:15–31

I consider that the sufferings of this present time are not worth comparing with the glory about to be revealed to us.

Romans 8:18 (NRSV)

My great-grandpa's wrinkles deepen when he chuckles. His blue eyes reflect a schoolboy's mischievous sense of humour. Nearly 100 years of living, through personal tragedies and historic disasters, have shaped my great-grandpa's perspective.

He listens to my frustrations with an occasional nod. Great-grandpa's response reflects the gentleness that often comes with age. 'Well…' signals his turn to talk. He pauses to complete his thought before putting it to words. My worries for the day will be fleeting thoughts, he assures me. He's not minimising my concerns; he just has a different perspective. His wisdom and peace of mind come from having always found God faithful.

Our Creator's perspective goes back much further than Great-grandpa's. It didn't start in 1913; God's perspective has always existed; it's eternal. God doesn't minimise our struggles but sees them in the light of eternity. God doesn't minimise our pain, but sees it in the light of eternal glory. When we cannot understand why God isn't working as we ask, scripture encourages us to trust.

Prayer: *Thank you, Father, that you are not limited to the human perspective of time. Remind us of your wisdom and love, and deepen our trust in you. Amen*

Thought for the day: When we trust God's perspective we can experience God's peace.

Jodi Schumm (Ohio, US)

The Whole Person

Read Psalm 8

[Mortals] look on the outward appearance, but the Lord looks on the heart.

1 Samuel 16:7 (NRSV)

When I was a teenager, I started falling in love; but I worried. Would anyone accept a disabled person like me? I kept praying and hoping for someone who would love me as I am, even as I passed my 30s and my 40s with no sign of a man who would accept me. My wish for a kind-hearted prince who would sweep me off my feet was just a dream.

I'm afraid of living alone for the rest of my life. I wonder, 'Doesn't God want me to marry while the feelings inside me are still burning?' I've tried to be social and to be confident, thinking that I am the same as other people. Finally, I've come to understand and accept that human beings see and judge others by their appearance and often do not look to see the whole person.

To human eyes I may be nothing, but God has created me valuable and unique. I am precious in God's eyes (Isaiah 43:4). By realising this, I feel happy doing my daily activities and having faith in God's promise that one day everything will be made beautiful (Ecclesiastes 3:11). Now I am sure, whether I get married or not, that I will always serve and honour God in everything I do.

Prayer: *Though to human eyes we may be of little worth, we know, Lord, that in your eyes we are infinitely valuable. Thank you for creating us and blessing us. Amen*

Thought for the day: Whatever our condition, God loves us.

Lautan Asima Basaria Siregar (Jakarta, Indonesia)

Say Thank You

Read Luke 17:11–19

[One of the ten lepers] threw himself at Jesus' feet and thanked him.
Luke 17:16 (NIV)

One evening recently I took my mother to hospital because she had a severe headache and her blood pressure was extremely high. A doctor checked her, reviewed her medical records and prescribed medication to lower her blood pressure. After the nurse had administered the medication, my mother's condition improved. When the doctor returned to check on her and to release her from the hospital, my mother said, 'I want to thank you for helping me tonight.'

The doctor replied, 'That's a first, and I appreciate it. Most people say, "When can I get out of here?" '

This event reminded me of the story of the ten lepers. Jesus told them to show themselves to the priests and they would be healed. All ten were healed, but only one returned to thank Jesus and to glorify God.

Too often, we take our blessings for granted. We're too busy or we don't care enough to thank God or to thank others for all they do for us. Psalm 92:1 says, 'It is a good thing to give thanks unto the Lord (KJV). I am grateful for the example my mother set. I want to be more like her and like the leper who was genuinely thankful, and took the time to thank Jesus for healing him.

Prayer: *Thank you, God, for always taking care of us and for giving us all that's good in our lives (see James 1:17). Amen*

Thought for the day: Take time daily to say thank you to God and to people who help you.

Janice Weatherly Williams (Georgia, US)

Come and Get It!

Read 2 Corinthians 2:14–17

Thanks be to God, who in Christ always leads us in triumphal procession, and through us spreads in every place the fragrance that comes from knowing him.

2 Corinthians 2:14 (NRSV)

We like to grill our food outside on the barbeque. We experiment with different ways of cooking: over an open flame, sometimes basting the meat with sweet teriyaki sauce, sometimes flavouring it with a zesty herb rub, and sometimes slowly smoking the food using hickory and apple-wood chips. Regardless of the method, we soon begin to smell the smoke and aroma in our back garden and beyond. When our guests arrive, they exclaim, 'What's that wonderful smell? Is that our dinner? We could smell it as soon as we got to your house!' It's an unmistakable fragrance. And we are thrilled when they ask us after dinner, 'Can we have the recipe? We'd like to make this for ourselves.'

Like our guests, being drawn by the aroma of the barbeque, people are drawn to God by the message of love. Our actions are meant to spread the good news of this love everywhere.

Prayer: *Loving God, give us the knowledge, wisdom and courage to be your arms and legs here on earth as we spread the good news of your love for each of us. Amen*

Thought for the day: What do my neighbours know about God's love because of knowing me?

Louise Anderson (California, US)

PRAYER FOCUS: EVANGELISTS

Thirst Quencher

Read John 7:37–39

Jesus said, 'Let anyone who is thirsty come to me, and... drink.'
John 7:37–38 (NRSV)

Years ago, I visited Ooty, a hill station in South India. The bus stopped for a while at a hairpin bend because the engine was overheated. The arduous journey had made us thirsty and hungry.

As I got off the bus and looked around, I saw water trickling from a crack in a big rock. It trickled into a bamboo pipe and collected in a wooden drum. I drank the cool, sweet water and quenched my thirst. The water was so satisfying that I decided not to eat anything that night but just fill my belly with the water that to me was as sweet as 'honey from the rock' (Psalm 81:16).

This incident reminded me of the living water that Jesus offers us. As we travel through life, we come across many hurdles and difficulties. We may be tempted to try to satisfy our spiritual thirst in many ways. But only a close relationship with God offers real, lasting satisfaction. Only God's living water can quench our soul's thirst.

Prayer: *Dear God, the world is thirsty for you. Thank you for sending Jesus to quench our thirst. May all those who are weary come to you as we pray, 'Our Father which art in heaven, Hallowed be thy name. Thy kingdom come. Thy will be done, as in heaven, so in earth. Give us day by day our daily bread. And forgive us our sins; for we also forgive every one that is indebted to us. And lead us not into temptation; but deliver us from evil.'* Amen*

Thought for the day: Christ offers living water freely to all.

Link2Life: *Go to www.upperroom.org for information on how to help provide clean water to families in need.*

Vincent Roop Singh (Bangalore, India)

 PRAYER FOCUS: THOSE WITHOUT ACCESS TO CLEAN WATER

* Luke 11:2–4 (KJV)

A Legacy

Read Proverbs 31:10–31

Paul wrote, 'I am reminded of your sincere faith, which first lived in your grandmother Lois and in your mother Eunice and, I am persuaded, now lives in you also.'

2 Timothy 1:5 (NIV)

I pulled out my sewing machine and sewing materials, brushing off 30 years' dust. With two granddaughters, I wanted to sew again for the first time in a long time. Pinning, cutting and stitching, it was as if my hands remembered the long dormant skills. But as I smoothed the fabric, I saw my grandmother's hands. When did my hands grow to look like hers?

I remember her hands sewing pearls onto my bridal veil, deftly kneading bread dough, sprinkling sugar and cinnamon on the best toast I've ever eaten. I remember her hands folded gracefully when I said my last goodbye to her so long ago.

I also remember her hands lifted in prayer. As a four-year-old, I sat by her side in her little church and saw her hands lifted toward heaven, her eyes closed, her lips moving as she talked to God. Watching her, I had no doubt that God was real and that God listened.

What a wonderful legacy she gave me! As I sew, I am sewing love into each stitch; I pray that I may also fashion for my granddaughters memories of my hands, helping, loving and praying.

Prayer: *Dear Lord, help each of us to leave a legacy of faith by the way we live every day. Amen*

Thought for the day: How can my actions today help others to see Christ?

Carol A. Lowe (Texas, US)

Forgiven and Clean

Read Psalm 103:7–18

As far as the east is from the west, so far has [the Lord] removed our transgressions from us.

Psalm 103:12 (NIV)

The sign above the 24-hour laundry/dry cleaner reads, 'Decent Cleaners'. This unusual name catches my attention each time I see it. Just what is the difference between decent and exceptional, decent and excellent, and decent and extraordinary? Why would I want my clothes to be laundered just 'decently'? Why shouldn't they be extraordinarily clean or exceptionally clean? Who is satisfied with merely decent? Am I asking too much if I desire excellence?

But in a spiritual sense, I consider what level of clean God can accomplish. Psalm 51:7 says, 'Wash me and I will be whiter than snow.' I think of 'whiter than snow' as exceptionally white, clean from top to bottom; for clothes, inside and out, pockets and cuffs, hidden linings and front lapels. The Bible tells us that every sin can be forgiven; every spot on the heart can be removed, to remove the stain of guilt on our soul.

Our own attempts to wash away our shame or cover our sin cannot succeed. But the forgiveness God offers is exceptional, excellent, extraordinary and thorough. I need to be cleaned of the guilt and released from the power of sin, and only God can do that. Each of us can confess our failures to God in prayer and be cleansed and forgiven.

Prayer: *Dear God, when we try and fail to live sinless lives, remind us that you can and will completely forgive all of our sins. Amen*

Thought for the day: Only God can wash away the stain of sin.

Sharon Braner (Oklahoma, US)

Outstretched Hand

Read Romans 7:5–25

[The Lord] drew me up from the desolate pit, out of the miry bog, and set my feet upon a rock, making my steps secure.

Psalm 40:2 (NRSV)

At the age of nine, I was running in my grandmother's garden and fell into an open rubbish dump that had filled with water during heavy rain. Somehow I managed to stretch my hand out. A person witnessing the incident grabbed my outstretched hand and rescued me. As soon as I was out of the pit, covered with putrid rubbish, people washed me and then provided medical care.

This incident reminds me of our human condition. Every day people fall into the pit of sin, and every day we also know that the hand of Christ is there to rescue us. Christ is waiting for us to stretch out our hand so he can save us, so he can wash our sins away. In the gospel story about Peter walking on the water, when Peter began to sink he cried out 'Lord, save me!' Immediately Jesus reached out his hand and saved him. Once I was heading to spiritual death in the deep and dirty pit of sin. Then Christ saved me. Alone I couldn't free myself from my dark and fatal situation, but by faith I reached out to take the hand of the Saviour.

Prayer: *Thank you, Lord, for reaching out to us and rescuing us from sin and its consequences. Amen*

Thought for the day: Sin is like putrid rubbish clinging to us, but God is always at hand to cleanse us and give new life.

Charlotte Mande Kasongo-Lenge (Cape Town, South Africa)

Labels and Categories

Read James 1:19–27

Be doers of the word, and not merely hearers who deceive themselves.
James 1:22 (NRSV)

An unpleasant feeling is spreading across our society and the world these days. Dialogue seems to have been replaced by name-calling that is little related to truth. Broadcasters fill the air with divisive labels designed to wound. Sometimes we see the same malice in the arena of faith and religion. This kind of talk reduces difficult issues to slogans and stops us from seeing others as worthwhile individuals. However, each of us has the choice and ability to move beyond labels and categories.

What changed for me is meeting people who are different from me. I discovered that they have hopes and dreams like mine. My study of scripture revealed that all people are of sacred worth. I learned that labels and categories can be used to lie and hide the truth, to injure and wound, to create fear and manipulate people. Words that make us suspicious of anyone who is different can make people into adversaries and enemies.

We read in Hebrews 13:1–2, 'Let mutual love continue. Do not neglect to show hospitality to strangers, for by doing that some have entertained angels without knowing it.' This counsel allows no exceptions. Any label or category that diminishes the worth of another person also diminishes us. As believers in Christ, we are called to honour every individual we meet as a person of sacred worth—nothing less.

Prayer: *O God, help us to love and respect one another as your children. In Jesus' name we pray. Amen*

Thought for the day: What labels limit my honouring people as God's beloved children?

F. Richard Garland (New Hampshire, US)

 PRAYER FOCUS: POLITICAL ADVERSARIES

Untethered

Read 1 Corinthians 15:50–57

I know that I will soon put [this body] aside, as our Lord Jesus Christ has made clear to me.

2 Peter 1:14 (NIV)

Recently my mother died in the intensive care unit of our local hospital, after struggling tenaciously for several weeks to hold on to life. While I prayed and read the Bible to her, she suffered what seemed to be a massive stroke that shook her body as a violent storm can shake a tent. A few seconds later, her body relaxed in peace. It was as if someone removed the main pole of a tent and allowed it to slowly billow to the ground.

A few minutes later the medical staff removed the tubes and wires that tethered my mother to earthly existence. Her life here on earth was over. But her soul was freed from the grip of pain and suffering.

I realised that the body is only a 'tent' which will be loosed from the earth and put off as our day clothes are when night comes. Like my mother, we who know Christ have hope for eternal life where the storms of this life can no longer batter and shake our earthly tent. What an indescribable gift!

Prayer: *Dear God, thank you for the promise of eternal life in your loving presence. Amen*

Thought for the day: Death is the passage to enter eternal life and peace.

John Warrener (Georgia, US)

Salvation's Way

Read John 3:16–21

Jesus said, 'I am the way and the truth and the life. No one comes to the Father except through me.'

John 14:6 (NIV)

My daughter was playing in a netball tournament out of town. Unsure of how to get there, I e-mailed several parents asking for directions. Within a few hours, I received several replies. I expected all the directions to be the same, but each person had mapped out a different route to the courts. Each claimed to be sending advice about the best and fastest way to get there, but after reading them I was more confused than before.

In contrast to the directions I received, the way to relationship with God is not at all confusing. Jesus said, 'I am the way and the truth and the life. No one comes to the Father except through me' (John 14:6). To develop an eternal relationship with God, we follow Jesus. That seems simple.

However, our journey to a deep relationship with God is not easy. This journey calls us to focus on the path set before us and to seek direction from God through daily prayer, Bible study, worship and Christian fellowship. Following God's direction can be challenging. But by fixing our eyes on Jesus Christ, accepting him as our Lord and Saviour, and choosing to follow his path of love and obedience, we will reach our final destination.

Prayer: *Thank you, Lord, for salvation and eternal relationship with you. Guide us to focus on your word and to obey your will. Amen*

Thought for the day: What helps me to find direction from God?

Denise Lewis (Florida, US)

The Missing Piece

Read 1 Corinthians 13

Love never fails.

1 Corinthians 13:8 (NIV)

I enjoy assembling furniture that comes in 'flat packs'. All the pieces are delivered in a flat box; and by reading the instructions carefully, I can build the furniture. The chairs I intended to make seemed fairly easy. I read the instructions carefully and laid out the components in the correct order. After a few false starts, I had three of the chairs assembled and ready for use. But I had a problem with the fourth chair. One of the smallest screws was missing from the pack. I searched everywhere but couldn't find it. Without it, the chair couldn't be completed and would not be safe to use. I phoned the help line, and soon the needed screw was dispatched to me. When it arrived, I completed the assembly and the chair was ready for use. One tiny piece made all the difference.

My experience with the chairs reminded me of our serving God. Whatever gifts we have, however strong our faith or generous our giving, none of these count without the presence of a loving spirit. Out of love, Jesus went to the cross, and Love raised him from the grave. Love is the essential ingredient.

Prayer: *O God, help us to serve our neighbours in love. Amen*

Thought for the day: 'Above all, clothe yourselves with love, which binds everything together in perfect harmony' (Colossians 3:14, NRSV).

Carol Purves (Cumbria, England)

Beyond Hope

Read Lamentations 3:19–26

The Lord is good to those whose hope is in him, to the one who seeks him; it is good to wait quietly for the salvation of the Lord.
Lamentations 3:25–26 (NIV)

A hundred miles south of our home is a tiny desert town called Hope. Those who drive through Hope in winter see hundreds of vehicles. For four months of the year, the town becomes home to visitors escaping the cold. Those who drive through the town in the summer see a main street that is mostly boarded up. But winter or summer, the last thing visitors see as they drive out of the town is a sign proclaiming, 'You're now out of Hope.'

I would not like to be told on a daily basis that I am beyond hope or that all hope is behind me. On some days, I feel that my life could hardly be worse; but with God, I can always have hope.

The writer of Lamentations was in a desperate place, feeling broken, besieged and surrounded by hardship with no way of escape. Forsaken and helpless, in the middle of the lament in chapter 3 the prophet does an about-face and declares a message of hope, choosing to focus on the One whose love gives us hope. Our hope today has the same basis: 'Because of the Lord's great love we are not consumed, for his compassions never fail. They are new every morning' (Lamentations 3:22–23).

Prayer: *O God, even when we feel desperate, help us to find hope in your great love and never-failing compassion. Amen*

Thought for the day: Those who lean on God's love always have reason for hope.

Joy P. Gage (Arizona, US)

Remembering God's Promises

Read Psalm 145:8–19

The Lord your God is with you, he is mighty to save. He will take great delight in you, he will quiet you with his love, he will rejoice over you with singing.

Zephaniah 3:17 (NIV)

During our Bible study the leader handed me three sheets of Bible verses with instructions to memorise one verse every month. As I read them, one verse especially comforted me: Zephaniah 3:17. A few days before our meeting, my doctor had informed me that I had a tumour in the membrane covering my brain, and that I would need surgery. The verse from Zephaniah quoted above reminded me of God's power and love in the midst of my anxiety.

I repeated the verse as a machine took pictures of my brain. I remembered its words when I was in hospital and whenever I lay awake in the night. Each time, God 'quieted me with his love'. During my long recovery, I remembered the words 'God is with you.'

God's word from the prophet Zephaniah encouraged me at a difficult time. I was able to think about God and his love and goodness instead of worrying about circumstances I could not change.

Memorising scripture allows us to take it with us everywhere we go so that whatever circumstances arise, we can find strength and encouragement from God who delights in us.

Prayer: *Dear God, thank you for your holy messages in scripture. Help us to remember your promises to us. Amen*

Thought for the day: 'Let the word of Christ dwell in you richly' (Colossians 3:16).

Yvonne E. Albright (Michigan, US)

PRAYER FOCUS: THOSE UNDERGOING SURGERY

The Way Out

Read Luke 24:13–32

While they were talking and discussing, Jesus himself came near and went with them, but their eyes were kept from recognising him.
Luke 24:15–16 (NRSV)

Our family was enjoying a holiday at a theme park. Suddenly my wife and I noticed that our small son was missing. Greatly alarmed, we began searching for him. Someone told us to check the maze created by a series of hedges. We climbed a platform that allowed us to see its entire layout. With great relief and joy, we saw our son—lost within the maze and frightened. From our vantage point we could see him, but our son's focus was on finding the way out. He was so afraid that he couldn't recognise us or even see us. But soon we were together again, and we could comfort him.

This experience brought to mind the Bible passage that tells how, after the resurrection, Jesus walked with two of the disciples who failed to recognise him. They heard his voice and saw his face, yet their vision was clouded and they failed to discern who he was.

Sometimes we find ourselves in similar circumstances. Faced with challenges, we become disillusioned and uncertain. Then Christ appears, offering guidance and hope to us. Even in the depths of our distress, Christ continues to walk by our side, hold our hand and guide us until we find the way out.

Prayer: *Loving God, draw near us when we become disoriented. Show us the path you want us to take. Amen*

Thought for the day: When we feel lost, God is present to guide us.

Luis Alberto Jones (Chubut, Argentina)

 PRAYER FOCUS: PARENTS AND FAMILIES OF MISSING CHILDREN

No Regrets

Read Philippians 3:7–15

If we confess our sins, he who is faithful and just will forgive us our sins and cleanse us from all unrighteousness.

1 John 1:9 (NRSV)

A great man and religious leader whom I admired often said that he had lived his entire life with no regrets. However, as I reflect on my choices, I have many regrets that trouble me. I have spent countless hours reflecting on words I said, decisions I made, or actions I took that I wish I could 'un-do'.

John wrote, 'If we confess our sins, he who is faithful and just will forgive us our sins and cleanse us from all unrighteousness.' I realise that not all of the actions I regret are necessarily sins but rather some are unwise choices or errors in judgment. For example, I once decided to take a job many miles from my home and family, a job that kept me from participating in the joy of birthdays and many other parts of family life. For both sins and errors, God's message is the same: It does no one good to look back and wonder what if... or if only I....

I have learned that to lead a good life—a God-centred life—it is not important to have no regrets. When I reflect on the past but keep my eyes on the future, I can see some value even in the things I regret. Our experiences, especially the mistakes we have made, can serve to make us stronger and wiser.

Prayer: *Dear Lord God, help us to rest in your loving arms and know that your love for us is bigger than all our regrets. In Jesus' name. Amen*

Thought for the day: We can leave past actions and regrets in the loving hands of God.

Jack Cameron (North Carolina, US)

PRAYER FOCUS: THOSE WORKING FAR FROM FAMILY

Vegetables and Fruit

Read Luke 13:6–9

'Sir,' the man replied, 'leave [the tree] alone for one more year, and I'll dig around it and fertilise it.'

Luke 13:8 (NIV)

I remember the time someone gave me some exceptional home-grown vegetables. While thanking the people involved, I asked what had made the vegetables so good. They told me that the growing temperature had been just right and it had rained at just the right time. Much of what led to their exceptional crop did not depend on them.

Unlike that vegetable crop, much of what influences our spiritual life does depend upon us. We determine our attitude, our disciplines and our willingness to grow. So I check myself from time to time. I look at my attitudes: do I trust God? Am I seeking to stay in love with God? I look at my spiritual practices: praying, reading the Bible, attending worship, receiving Communion, doing all the good I can, avoiding all the evil I can. Do I seek out spiritual counsel? I look at my willingness to grow: do I desire God above all things?

I want to bear exceptional fruit in God's kingdom, but I know that means I cannot simply depend on what comes to me. I have my part to do.

Prayer: *Dear God, we want to bear good fruit. Help us to feed our souls by taking advantage of the means of grace you provide. As Jesus taught us, we pray, 'Our Father in heaven, hallowed be your name, your kingdom come, your will be done on earth as it is in heaven. Give us today our daily bread. Forgive us our debts, as we also have forgiven our debtors. And lead us not into temptation, but deliver us from the evil one.'* Amen*

Thought for the day: We are partners with God in the fruit-bearing business.

Bradford Reeves (Texas, US)

 PRAYER FOCUS: THOSE STRUGGLING TO GROW IN GOD'S GRACE

* Matthew 6:9–13 (NIV)

Starting the Day

Read Psalm 150:1–6

It is good to give thanks to the Lord, to sing praises to your name, O Most High; to declare your steadfast love in the morning, and your faithfulness by night.

Psalm 92:1–2 (NRSV)

Some time ago while staying in a mission guesthouse in Ethiopia, my husband and I woke one morning to the sound of five or six voices singing a hymn. What a delightful start for our day! The sound came from a large room close to ours; and not long afterwards, when I met the family at breakfast, I told them how much we had appreciated their singing.

'We always like to begin the day that way,' the mother explained.

I thought about her words as we travelled home to our own mission station; and soon afterwards, my husband and I decided to start our day with a praise song too. We used a large hymnbook that friends had given us at the start of our mission assignment. We have sung a morning hymn together ever since. Doing so lifts our thoughts to God before we go on to read the Bible and to pray.

I'm glad that, quite unintentionally, a family introduced us to this simple yet uplifting start for each day. What can you do to begin your days with a sense of God's presence and love?

Prayer: *Dear Lord, when we think of all you have done and will yet do for us, we are filled with the joy of praising you. Amen*

Thought for the day: Any time of day is a good time to praise God.

Elaine Brown (Perthshire, Scotland)

Real Giving

Read Mark 12:41–44

'She gave all she had to live on.'

Mark 12:44 (GNB)

I was part of a medical team working in Haiti at the time of the earthquake in January 2010. During my time there, I learned about real giving. One day my son and I were playing soccer with Haitian children. During a break, we handed out some caramels. One of the boys bit his caramel in half and offered one half to me. I was on my way to eat more than this boy would get in several days, yet he offered me half of what he had.

Our team continued operating the medical clinic after the earthquake, but it wasn't clear how or when we were going home. We decided that we should begin conserving our food as well as our fuel for the generators. One of our interpreters said he would bring us food from his home if we needed any. He and his five children live in a house smaller than most of our living rooms, and we had more food in our kitchen than his family would eat in two months. His ability to provide food for his own family would soon be in question. Yet he offered us a gift beyond measure. He knew about real giving.

God calls us to be generous stewards of all our gifts. How are you doing that?

Prayer: *O God, move us to give to you all we can—in serving and in sharing our resources. Amen*

Thought for the day: Whatever we have, God calls us to give generously to those with less.

Link2Life: *Go to www.umcor.org to learn about relief efforts in Haiti.*

Bruce Blumer (South Dakota, US)

To Show the World

Read John 17:20–26

'You will receive power when the Holy Spirit comes on you; and you will be my witnesses in Jerusalem, in all Judea and Samaria, and to the ends of the earth.'

Acts 1:8 (NIV)

Jesus was a travelling rabbi. When he called people to follow him, they had to leave their life as it was and go God-only-knew-where. How hard it must have been for the disciples to leave their families, their work, the life they knew, to follow Jesus, whose only road map was the voice of God! And in the end, Jesus was moving without them: 'Where I am going, you cannot come,' he says (John 13:33). 'I am going… to prepare a place for you… that you also may be where I am' (John 14:2–3).

What good news does John want the Church to hear in Jesus' message? First, assurance that the Holy Spirit will be with them. Jesus tells his disciples, 'It is to your advantage that I go away, for if I… go, I will send [the Advocate] to you' (John 16:7, NRSV). At Pentecost, the Holy Spirit came so that the Church could be Jesus' presence in his absence.

Second, Jesus prays that his disciples will be unified. He prays that they will show the world what sacrificial love can do. Jesus prays that they and we will be faithful to the way, truth and life that he has demonstrated. Jesus prays that as he and the Father are one, so we all would be bound together in Christian love, no matter where the Holy Spirit leads us.

Prayer: *Dear God, give us the courage to follow you. Thank you for our companions along the way. Amen*

Thought for the day: When we have to move, let's move with God.

Mike Ripski (Tennessee, US)

The Prince of Our Peace

Read Isaiah 9:2–7

To us a child is born, to us a son is given, and the government will be on his shoulders. And he will be called Wonderful Counsellor, Mighty God, Everlasting Father, Prince of Peace.

Isaiah 9:6 (NIV)

While living in Louisville, Kentucky, I visited a military cemetery. White crosses were everywhere, all alike, perfectly aligned. I walked among them, reading inscriptions. One young man died when he was only 19; another died in his 20s; a young woman died at 26. Tears streamed down my face as I thought of the lives lost, of widows and children left behind, of sons and daughters who never came home. I was overwhelmed with sorrow, knowing how such loss must grieve God.

Our world desperately needs peace and God wants it for us. We need nations to reconcile and wars to cease. The huge amounts of money spent on war could be used to provide healthcare, food, shelter for the needy and jobs for those able to work. We also need peace in our homes, homes where people love and respect each other, and learn to love God and others. And we need peace in our hearts. Many of us are filled with guilt, fear and worry; but we need not be. Jesus Christ, the Prince of Peace, offers peace to all who will receive it.

Prayer: *Dear God, bring peace on earth and within us. Amen*

Thought for the day: Let us pray and work for peace.

Robert G. Wilkerson (Alabama, US)

Keeping the Air-Line Clear

Read Psalm 51

Keep your servant... from wilful sins; may they not rule over me.
Psalm 19:13 (NIV)

During the regular late-night check of the Seahorse and Fish farm, one tank was discovered to have an airflow problem. The fish were lethargic, and if the problem was not solved by morning, they would be dead. Checking the air-line revealed the problem: small particles of salt from the water had come together and over time had choked the flow. After a simple clean, the air flowed freely and the fish were safe.

I see in this a parable. To live a healthy, happy, godly life requires open lines of communication between us and God. Living as we do in a sinful world, indifferent to Christ, it is easy for our spiritual lifeline to become clogged. Unhealthy attitudes, an unforgiving spirit and unwholesome images leave particles in our soul without our realising it. Slowly, surely, our spiritual freshness is strangled. But, unlike the fish in that tank, we can do something about our situation. We can cry out to our Lord to keep the spiritual lifeline clear: 'Have mercy on me, O God, according to your unfailing love... Wash away all my iniquity and cleanse me from my sin' (Psalm 51:1–2).

Prayer: *Dear Lord, make us sensitive to anything that blocks our relationship with you. Keep us clear, we pray. Amen*

Thought for the day: A holy life depends on an open line to God.

Raymond N. Hawkins (Tasmania, Australia)

Quiet Wisdom

Read Psalm 32:1–7

Hear, my child, your father's instruction, and do not reject your mother's teaching.

Proverbs 1:8 (NRSV)

My parents had gone shopping. As I stood alone in Mum and Dad's bedroom and my grandmother was napping in another part of the house, I noticed a box of matches on my Dad's bedside table. As I picked up the box, I could hear in my mind my father's voice saying as he had many times, 'Don't play with matches!' Behind the table were lovely white curtains. What would happen if I struck a match and touched the curtain quickly? A small hole appeared in the curtain. I was horrified and quickly tucked the curtain behind the table. Maybe they would never see it.

That night as I got in bed and pulled the covers over me, my stomach began to hurt. It got worse, and I wept. My father came to me and asked, 'What's the matter?'

I said, 'I have a bad stomach-ache.'

My father sat quietly by my side, 'Where does it hurt?'

He put his strong hand on my chest and asked, 'Does it feel like a burned curtain?' Then he said, 'I think you have learned your lesson. I love you. Now get some sleep.'

My stomach-ache immediately stopped. My conscience was clean. I never forgot my father's quiet wisdom. Through the years as I have grown in my faith, I have come to understand that God's love and forgiveness clear the conscience.

Prayer: *Dear God, thank you for the wonder of forgiveness and the freedom it brings. Thank you for being ready to forgive us even before we ask. Amen*

Thought for the day: God cleanses every repentant heart.

Woody A. Adams (North Carolina, US)

Both Ways

Read John 7:37–38

Freely you have received, freely give.

Matthew 10:8 (NIV)

Centuries ago the native people living alongside what is now known as the Hudson River had their own name for this stream of water. They called it Muh-he-kun-ne-tuk, 'The River that Flows Both Ways'. When the tide from the Atlantic Ocean flows into this waterway, the river flows north; and when the tide goes out, the river flows south.

When I learned about this, I realised that it holds a lesson for us: what flows into our life from God is meant to flow out from it. We're to have in our heart a river that flows both ways: God's love flows in, and it is meant to flow out. I experience the tide of God's grace, and then I show grace—graciousness—to others. I'm forgiven, and I forgive others. God's strength streams in, and I'm to build up others. The presence of Christ floods my soul, and from my heart is to flow that same divine presence. Each of us can have within us a river that flows two ways.

Prayer: *Dear Father, as you have filled us with your grace and mercy and love, help us to share with others. We pray as Jesus taught us, saying, 'Our Father which art in heaven, Hallowed be thy name. Thy kingdom come. Thy will be done in earth, as it is in heaven. Give us this day our daily bread. And forgive us our debts, as we forgive our debtors. And lead us not into temptation, but deliver us from evil: For thine is the kingdom, and the power, and the glory, for ever.'* Amen*

Thought for the day: As God blesses me, I am to bless others.

David T. De Hass (Iowa, US)

PRAYER FOCUS: NATIVE PEOPLES

* Matthew 6:9–13 (KJV)

Worth the Wait

Read Psalm 25:1–10

Show me your ways, O Lord, teach me your paths; guide me in your truth and teach me, for you are God my Saviour, and my hope is in you all day long.

Psalm 25:4–5 (NIV)

On my third telephone call I heard the same recorded message, 'Please wait for the next available representative.' Loud music began playing in my ear, and I wanted to slam the telephone down. I had waited seven or eight minutes on the first two calls without talking to a live person and had achieved nothing by waiting. Yet I knew I had to keep trying.

I have often found it difficult to wait, to be patient in situations where I have no control. I have allowed frustration and impatience to block me in reaching my objectives and following my plans. In so doing, I have no doubt squandered opportunities to attain a goal and serve others.

It has taken me considerable time to see that God's timing seldom matches my expectations. As I reflect on God's faithfulness and perfect wisdom, I am reminded with each step of faith that I can turn my impatience, worries, even my failures, over to the Lord. We have this promise from the prophet Isaiah: 'Yet the Lord longs to be gracious to you; he rises to show you compassion... Blessed are all who wait for him' (30:18). I am finding that the more I wait for and depend upon the Lord, the easier it is to respond in trying situations 'with patience and love'.

Prayer: *Thank you, Father, for your grace given freely to us. Forgive our impatience and heal any hurt that we have caused by acting on it. Amen*

Thought for the day: God rewards our patience with peace.

Walter N. Maris (Missouri, US)

 PRAYER FOCUS: THOSE TRYING TO BE MORE PATIENT

A Good Cup

Read Luke 22:17–20

Whenever you eat this bread and drink this cup, you proclaim the Lord's death until he comes.

1 Corinthians 11:26 (NIV)

As I prepared to take the night shift in driving to visit our families for the holidays, I realised that I really needed a good cup of coffee—the kind my grandpa used to make for me when I was a child, containing as much cream and sugar as coffee. And I think of the wonderful man who made it for me—memories of his love, laughter and teasing.

Whenever we partake of the Lord's Supper, we remember someone we love. We see Jesus looking into the eyes of his friends as he handed them the bread and cup and said, 'Remember me!' (see Luke 22:19). I wonder if they remembered his face every time they broke the bread. Or did they miss his look of love as he passed the cup to each of them? Later, were they as overwhelmed with missing Jesus as I was with missing my grandpa as I drove along drinking my coffee in the wee hours of the morning?

Even 35 years after Grandpa's death, a good cup of coffee brings back memories of sitting on his knee. Our times of Holy Communion now are much more powerful cups of remembrance of the One who gave his all for us and who asked us to remember him.

Prayer: *Dear God, thank you for loving us more than anyone on earth ever could. Amen*

Thought for the day: I can know Jesus and remember what he did for me.

Esther Rigsby (Singapore)

By the Stars

Read Isaiah 40:25–31

Magi from the east came to Jerusalem and asked, 'Where is the one who has been born king of the Jews? We saw his star in the east and have come to worship him.'

Matthew 2:1–2 (NIV)

While on a construction mission trip to a rural area of Panama, I awoke in the middle of the night. The moon had set, and millions of stars were clearly visible. It was an amazing sight. I looked north and easily recognised the North Star and identified the constellations that we call the Little Dipper and the Big Dipper. I then looked into the opposite sky and saw for the first time the Southern Cross. The brightness and clarity of this constellation was amazing; it was a spiritual moment. For me the message was clear: follow the cross.

For centuries travellers (especially sailors) have navigated by the stars to find their way. Christians have been given an even more reliable navigation system—not the stars but the Bible. If we look to its stories and live by its wisdom, the Bible can guide us to 'follow the cross' day by day.

Prayer: *Dear Lord, thank you for the light you provide for our journey. Give us the power, courage and wisdom to follow your guidance in our daily walk of faith. Amen*

Thought for the day: If we look, we will find in the Bible daily guidance and direction.

Dick Clarke (South Carolina, US)

Children of God

Read 1 John 3:1–3

How great is the love the Father has lavished on us, that we should be called children of God!

1 John 3:1 (NIV)

The day with my four-year-old had been particularly trying. I was tired and felt like a failure. When I looked in on her before going to bed myself, I stood for a while, watching her sleep peacefully. While breathing in the fresh scent of her, I thought of the trials of the day and of my love for her. Earlier I had lost my patience and been frustrated, but my frustration could never diminish my love for her. I gently stroked her face and whispered, 'I will always love you. Tomorrow will be a better day.'

It suddenly occurred to me that God loves me the way I love my daughter—but immeasurably more than we humans could ever be capable of. I am a child of God. Even when I frustrate God and fail to listen, God's love endures. I may make mistakes, but God will always smile on me with unending love. I imagine God, looking down on me as I sleep and saying, 'I will always love you. Tomorrow will be a better day.'

That night I was able to go to sleep full of hope for the next day.

Prayer: *Dear heavenly Father, thank you for loving us unconditionally. May we convey your love to our families and to those we encounter throughout our days. Amen*

Thought for the day: I am a dearly loved child of God.

Victoria Kubasak (California, US)

Getting to Know You

Read John 10:1–18

Jesus said, 'I know my sheep and my sheep know me.'

John 10:14 (NIV)

For the past 16 years I have been attending a Bible study group for women. We gather for a small meal followed by discussion and end by praying for one another.

Recently, the leader of our group was diagnosed with cancer. After surgery she was told she would be having 18 weeks of chemotherapy. Because she lives alone and has no close relatives, we in the Bible study group took turns to stay with her. We prepared her meals and accompanied her to chemotherapy treatments.

One day she said to me, 'I thought I knew you all, but during these last few months I really got to know each one of you as we spent time together one-to-one. This has been a real blessing. I felt comfortable with you all, and lovingly "held" by you as I went through the treatment.'

Isn't that the same with Christ? We don't really know his character and experience his goodness, mercy, love and power until we spend time with him. As we read the Bible and relax in Christ's company, Christ holds us in love and heals us.

Prayer: *Dear God, help us to spend time with you so that we can come to know you better and have a deeper relationship with you. Amen*

Thought for the day: The gift of time is a gift of love.

Joan Kangalee (London, England)

A Garden of Hope

Read Mark 11:22–25

Jesus said, 'Whatever you ask for in prayer, believe that you have received it, and it will be yours.'

Mark 11:24 (NIV)

In South Africa, while working at a shelter that housed boys who had previously lived and worked on the streets, I was surrounded by poverty, neglect, addiction and filth. The children I worked with knew little about beauty or the magnificence of God and creation. So one day I decided to plant a garden. With the help of the children, I planted lilies, marigolds, violets, dianthus, peonies and several kinds of lush, green grasses.

After we had finished, I prayed for our garden to take shape and grow, even in this unusually hard African dirt and clay. I believed we could bring beauty to the children through these flowers. Soon, the lilies were the largest I had ever seen; the orange marigolds glowed with colour set against the red dianthus; the peonies opened and so did the hearts of the children. They found joy in our little garden of hope.

Sometimes we may think certain prayer requests are too small for God to deal with. In the midst of working with children dealing with great pain and suffering, I prayed for a garden. I am reminded of God's answer to this prayer daily; and I'm spurred on in faith, knowing that God is always faithful and always listens.

Prayer: *Dear God, thank you for the beauty of creation. We love you for your faithfulness and for your answers to prayer. In Jesus' name. Amen*

Thought for the day: No concern is too small to bring to God.

Link2Life: *To see a photo of Megan and the children in their garden, go to www.upperroom.org.*

Megan Daniso (Oregon, US)

Our Bleakest Moments

Read Romans 8:26–30

The Spirit helps us in our weakness; for we do not know how to pray as we ought, but that very Spirit intercedes with sighs too deep for words.
Romans 8:26 (NRSV)

The family I grew up in was dysfunctional. Because my childhood was so chaotic and void of balance or security, I spent my early adulthood chasing my own personal gods. I pursued acceptance, perfection and unconditional love through my relationships with colleagues, friends and loved ones. I judged everyone, including myself, by how they lived up to my standards for behaviour. Rarely were my judgments positive.

The frustration of my search began to consume me, and along the way I began to drink. Many nights ended with me passing out in an alcoholic stupor. My life was in shambles. Eventually my wife left, taking our child; my marriage was all but over. But God, in his infinite mercy and grace, kept working in my life.

I gave my alcohol addiction over to God, asking for help, and he gave me a new life. Over the course of time, I found in relationship with him the acceptance and unconditional love that I had searched for all my life. Now, thanks to God, my marriage is stronger, our house is a home, and I have a church family that fills me with joy.

Prayer: *Dear Father, thank you for the grace and mercy you offer us. The healing power of your love knows no limits. We pray as Jesus taught us, saying, 'Father, hallowed be your name, your kingdom come. Give us each day our daily bread. Forgive us our sins, for we also forgive everyone who sins against us. And lead us not into temptation.'* Amen*

Thought for the day: Nothing the world offers can compare to the life God has in store for us.

Timothy Stepan (Texas, US)

 PRAYER FOCUS: ALCOHOLICS AND THEIR FAMILIES

* Luke 11:2–4 (NIV)

Return on Investment

Read Matthew 25:14–29

'Well done, good and faithful servant!'

Matthew 25:21 (NIV)

Every wise manager is looking for those who are good at what they do in order to put them in charge of more. It's a principle in life, isn't it? It's about effectiveness. In this passage from Matthew, Jesus speaks of this principle: responsible behaviour in small matters leads to having responsibility over more.

What are you responsible for? What does someone trust you to do today? Whatever it is, do it well—today, tomorrow and the next day. Trust is something we earn every day.

God entrusts each of us with many things—our work, our possessions, our time, our relationships. What kind of return is God getting on these from us? Part of the beauty of the Christian life is that the risen, living Christ longs to come into our lives. Christ wants to empower us to make faith-filled decisions that lead to positive returns, so that God's kingdom may grow in us and throughout the world.

We can live focused days, empowered by the indwelling Christ, choosing with his help to pay attention to what really matters. Then we will be able to hear God say, 'Well done, good and faithful servant!'

Prayer: *Gracious God, we want to be faithful in using the gifts you have given us. Strengthen us by the power of the indwelling Christ to live for you every day. Amen*

Thought for the day: What really matters is loving God and loving the people in our lives.

Dan G. Johnson (Florida, US)

Little Holes

Read Psalm 104:24–30

[O Lord], you search out my path and my lying down, and are acquainted with all my ways.

Psalm 139:3 (NRSV)

Early one spring morning, my three-year-old daughter and I were hurrying to her nursery school. Actually, I was hurrying and beginning to get irritated because my daughter was in no rush. When we were only a few yards from the gate of her school, I had to stop again. My daughter had turned aside and was bent over a piece of brick that was jutting out from the melting snow. I called her angrily. She came to me and walked the final few steps to the gate with tears in her eyes.

'Why are you crying?' I asked.

'I only wanted to look at the little holes,' she answered through her tears.

Little holes? At that moment, I felt as if a wave of God's presence had enveloped me. God is everywhere and in everything, even the little holes in that brick. In an instant all my irritation disappeared. I embraced my daughter and said, 'I'm sorry. I love you.' I was ashamed that my haste had been the cause of her tears. In the little holes of a brick, God had shown me an opportunity to love and opened my eyes to see more deeply into ordinary events.

Prayer: *Dear Lord, thank you for surrounding us with your gifts. Thank you for always being by our side and showing us the path to follow. In your love, help us to overcome the stress of life so that we never cause those we love to cry. Amen*

Thought for the day: Do I live in stress or in God's peace?

Irina Kurkina (Yetaterinburg, Russia)

The Same

Read John 1:1–5

Jesus Christ is the same yesterday and today and forever.
Hebrews 13:8 (NRSV)

How many times have you been told, 'You haven't changed a bit!' when you know full well that you have. In fact, you may have changed a lot. How can anyone from birth to now not change? Even though we may feel young at heart, we grow older. Whether from inside or outside forces, we change.

I am almost 80, and I cannot name all the changes I've experienced from primary to high-school, college and university, or from working as a primary- and high-school teacher and as a counsellor until retirement. My hair has changed from brown to grey. My home town has dwindled in population. The world seems smaller with new communication technologies. The population of the city where I now live has grown from thousands to over two million. The church I have attended since 1964 has changed; building renovations and changes of pastors are inevitable. Our hearts may grieve over change, but it has to be.

With all changes, however, we can thank God for our faith, a place to worship that is open to all, opportunities for Bible study, and a God who is ever present to lead, guide and fill us daily with love. Yet most of all I thank God for Jesus Christ, our Saviour, who remains the same.

Prayer: *Almighty God, thank you for your presence at all times, for your guidance, for unending love and for eternal life through Jesus Christ our Lord. Amen*

Thought for the day: Life's details change, but the love and truth of Christ are constant and unfailing.

Dinah Lee Tanner (Texas, US)

Patterns

Read Romans 12:1–8

Do not conform any longer to the pattern of this world, but be transformed by the renewing of your mind.

Romans 12:2 (NIV)

I remember seeing my mother carefully cutting piece after piece of fabric. Although an accomplished seamstress, she did not rely on her ideas or experience. Neither size nor shape of a single piece was random. Instead, each cut followed a pattern. Ignoring the pattern would result in an ill-fitting garment.

A strategy similar to following a pattern is key to living a life pleasing to our Lord. God provides patterns and longs for us to follow them. When building the lamp stands, Moses was instructed, 'See that you make them according to the pattern shown you on the mountain' (Exodus 25:40). He obeyed.

Another pattern for living was revealed to us in the person of Jesus. As with all matters of faith, however, a decision is involved. The scissors were in my mother's hand. She could easily have altered the outcome. Moses could have disobeyed. Jesus could have chosen not to go to the cross. When we are willing to die to self and faithfully follow the divine design to love and serve others we can be made into what God would have us become.

Prayer: *Thank you, Lord, for sending Jesus to show us how to live. In his name we pray. Amen*

Thought for the day: What God wants for us emerges as we choose to follow Christ's example.

Robert L. Stephens (Virginia, US)

Going South

Read Ephesians 4:17—5:2

The Lord God made a woman from the rib he had taken out of the man, and he brought her to the man... For this reason a man will leave his father and mother and be united to his wife, and they will become one flesh.

Genesis 2:22, 24 (NIV)

I had said goodbye to my parents and brothers and sisters and was in the car, beginning my 200-mile trek southward. I had made this journey many times before, to visit, but this time I was going to stay. I was getting married. My soon-to-be wife and I had met at college, in a town halfway between our two homes; now I was moving to her home town. I was leaving my parents' household so my wife and I could set up a new household. I was leaving their family to start my own family.

In some ways, our relationship to Jesus Christ is similar to a marriage. When people marry, they declare that their new spouse is now primary in their life. Likewise, when we live in relationship with Christ, we commit to making Jesus the most important person in our lives.

This doesn't happen overnight, but as we pray, study the Bible and serve alongside those who also love Christ, we become more like our Lord. When we begin this relationship, we leave our old way of life and begin something new. We leave our selfishness and our sin. We leave our old priorities and reorder our other relationships to give Christ first place in our lives. Following him takes precedence over anything and everyone else.

Prayer: *Dear Lord Jesus Christ, help us to give you first place in all our relationships and decisions. Amen*

Thought for the day: Following Jesus takes us on life's most important journey.

Steve Wilson (Ohio, US)

Royal Correspondence

Read Hebrews 4:14—5:10

Let us... approach the throne of grace with confidence, so that we may receive mercy and find grace to help us in our time of need.
Hebrews 4:16 (NIV)

It required weeks of careful work, but at last it was finished: my letter to Her Majesty, Queen Sofia of Spain. Writing on behalf of my employer, I had spent days meticulously planning the tone, content and organisation of the letter in Spanish. I made successive drafts until every sentence seemed precisely right. A Spanish friend ensured that the final version had no grammatical errors, and the Spanish ambassador reviewed the letter to see that it included the proper forms of address and royal titles.

This experience led me to reflect more soberly on how often I lose sight of the privilege of prayer. The amount of time, thought and attention I devote to approaching God's throne of grace is entirely disproportionate to the divine majesty of my King. If I took such care with a letter to the Queen of Spain, how much more reverence is due the Lord of creation?

When we pray, we communicate with a King who is far greater than any earthly monarch. However, for this communication, we don't need anyone to check our grammar. We don't need to send letters via an embassy. Instead, because of Christ's death and resurrection, we can approach God's throne in prayer at any time, in any circumstance.

Prayer: *O God, my King, we marvel at the access you have granted us to your heavenly throne. Keep us mindful of your majesty. Amen*

Thought for the day: Prayer is communication with the King of kings.

Tyler Fisher (Oxfordshire, England)

Spilled Milk

Read Matthew 5:21–25

If it is possible, so far as it depends on you, live peaceably with all.
Romans 12:18 (NRSV)

While running through the house, my son crashed into the kitchen table causing a large glass of chocolate milk to spill. He was immediately remorseful and hurried to clean up the mess as fast as he could. When he had finished cleaning up the final drops of milk and I thought about his response to the situation, I was impressed. Instead of complaining about the glass being too close to the edge of the table or coming up with some other excuse, he took responsibility for his actions. I was pleased.

We all make mistakes. I hope that when I make a mistake I can respond in the way my son did. When I say something offensive or do something that hurts another person, do I try to cover it up, ignore it or blame someone else? Or do I immediately take responsibility for my actions and seek to make things right? I wonder if God feels as I did when I saw how my son responded to the mess in our kitchen.

Wouldn't it be great to know that God is pleased with us because of the way we react to a mistake? I hope that the next time I 'spill milk' I will respond as my son did and clean up my mess quickly.

Prayer: *Dear heavenly Father, we pray that you will help us stay close to you and always admit our mistakes. Amen*

Thought for the day: God is always willing to help us clean up the messes we make.

Jay Wollenburg (Ohio, US)

Learning to Lean

Read 2 Corinthians 4:5–16

God who said, 'Let light shine out of darkness'… has shone in our hearts to give the light of the knowledge of the glory of God in the face of Jesus Christ.

2 Corinthians 4:6 (NRSV)

For most of my life, I thought I could do anything and had complete control of everything. As a young man, I built our first house and completely remodelled our second house with my own two hands—carpentry, plumbing, masonry, electrical—everything. As I progressed through life I had different jobs with one company that I usually handled with ease. Two years ago my wife's health started to deteriorate so I took over the housework and the cooking. I handled that OK, too, until she was confined to a nursing home. At that point, I lost control of everything. I became physically ill, and my doctor referred me to a therapist who suggested that I 'take it one day at a time' (see Matthew 6:34).

However, my real help came from God. My wife and I have been churchgoers together for 60 years. As teenagers we used to sing 'Come into my heart, Lord Jesus'. I started repeating the words to that song each night before I went to sleep and then asked Jesus to help me. And he did. I realise that Christ has been in my heart all these years; I just never asked him for help. I am deeply sorry that I waited 78 years to get the message. But I have it now. Leaning on Christ and turning to him continually in prayer has changed my life.

Prayer: *Dearest Lord Jesus, you are always in our heart and listen to our every thought. Remind us to talk to you every day. Amen*

Thought for the day: Today is a good day to lean on God.

Tommy R. Amidon (Michigan, US)

 PRAYER FOCUS: TO GIVE UP OUR DELUSION OF CONTROL

Our Father

Read Ephesians 3:14–19

I bow my knees before the Father, from whom every family in heaven and on earth takes its name.

Ephesians 3:14–15 (NRSV)

I've always viewed Father's Day as a marketing ploy to generate sales of gifts and cards. However, a strange and delightful thing happened just before Father's Day this year. I received a surprise Father's Day gift from a young man I hardly knew.

I called to thank him for the generous gift and asked him the reason for his sending me a Father's Day gift. He told me that he always bought a Father's Day present every year but his father had died since Father's Day the preceding year. He had bought the gift for me as a way of honouring the memory of his father.

This act of unexpected generosity made me ask myself how often we remember that we have a heavenly father who loves us more than we will ever understand. What is our daily response, our gift, in gratitude for this unlimited love? We honour God's role in our lives by loving others.

Prayer: *Our Father, giver of all good gifts (see James 1:17), teach us to respond to your unlimited love by loving others. Amen*

Thought for the day: 'Beloved, let us love one another, because love is from God' (1 John 4:7).

Link2Life: *Give a gift to honour someone important to you.*

Roland P. Rink (Gauteng, South Africa)

PRAYER FOCUS: FATHERS

Father's Day

Read Matthew 5:1–12

A father to the fatherless, a defender of widows, is God in his holy dwelling.

Psalm 68:5 (NIV)

Father's Day was fast approaching, filling me with apprehension. There would not be the usual Father's Day celebration at a restaurant, with conversation and laughter. My father had died during the year, just six weeks after he was diagnosed with cancer. Thinking of his absence churned the waves of grief as memories washed over me. I recalled the heart-wrenching sadness and resignation in my father's voice when he informed me he didn't think he was 'long for this world'.

I rejoice for my father's life in eternity, but I miss his physical presence in my life. Yet as I progress through the stages of grieving, I find solace in God's word. Matthew 5:4 comforts me as I read that those who mourn will be comforted. I am reassured by Psalm 30:5 that 'weeping may remain for a night, but rejoicing comes in the morning'. My sadness and anxiety on Father's Day led me to pray, and I asked God to help me cope with my feelings. God responded by leading me to Psalm 68:5, where I read that God is a 'father to the fatherless, a defender of widows'. I wept with gratitude.

Scripture opens the door to heal our brokenness by revealing to us God's truth and promises. Our heavenly Father will never leave us or forsake us (see Hebrews 13:5). God watches over us and guides us through our grief and mourning. I will never be fatherless on Father's Day; God has assured me of that.

Prayer: *O God, thank you for being our heavenly Father. We rest in your loving arms. Amen*

Thought for the day: God, our father, is and always will be with us.

Debra E. Pierce (Massachusetts, US)

 PRAYER FOCUS: THOSE MOURNING A FATHER'S DEATH

Goose Inspiration

Read James 1:2–5

Let us consider how we may spur one another on toward love and good deeds.

Hebrews 10:24 (NIV)

One morning during my routine jog for exercise, a goose joined me. I was surprised to see a lone goose far from a water source. When I had a few more laps to go, the goose began to honk and hiss as I passed. On my last lap, the grumpy bird was following behind me. Unlike other days when my last lap was my slowest and most difficult to complete, this day I finished my jog in a full run.

I still smile when I picture that goose trying to bully me. I could have let that squawking, bobbing fowl stop me or I could have changed my course. Instead, I chose to keep moving forward, focused on finishing my run even though I changed how I finished it. In this case, the squawking goose helped push me the little bit that I needed.

Likewise, God can use challenges in our lives to bolster our determination. As a teacher, I once had a very challenging student. When the school year ended, he slipped a note onto my desk: 'Thanks for not giving up.' That was the year God reignited my passion for teaching and equipped me for work at a school for troubled teenagers. Each obstacle we face can help to prepare us for the next stage of our spiritual journey.

Prayer: *Dear God of our deliverance, help us to overcome the challenges we will face on our physical and spiritual journeys. Amen*

Thought for the day: Even a grumpy goose can be used by God for good.

Teri Miller (Virginia, US)

PRAYER FOCUS: SPECIAL-EDUCATION TEACHERS

Not in Vain

Read 1 Peter 4:8–11

Stand firm. Let nothing move you. Always give yourselves fully to the work of the Lord, because you know that your labour in the Lord is not in vain.

1 Corinthians 15:58 (NIV)

As a single, full-time caregiver for an ageing parent with complex medical needs and memory loss, I have felt overwhelmed, frustrated and isolated. While caring church family and friends have offered to help, they have their own responsibilities demanding attention. One particular day was extremely trying for both my parent and me, leaving both of us in tears. I felt drained and hopeless and cried out to God seeking relief.

Early the next morning, a dear spiritual sister sent me a simple text message, 'You R loved by me.' Later, another sister called to say that she was thinking about me and praying for me. She mentioned the words of an old gospel hymn, encouraging me to hold on and to remember that my labour is not in vain. Finally, later in the day, a dear friend who is a pastor in another part of the country telephoned me to encourage me and pray with me.

I see these events not as coincidences but rather as clear signs that our loving God sees, hears and cares about our trials. The Lord encouraged me through my sisters and brother in Christ. They were God's presence to me.

Prayer: *Thank you, Lord, that you use for good every small act of obedience. Amen*

Thought for the day: Our small acts of caring can have great impact for those in need.

Link2Life: *Call a carer and offer to relieve them for an afternoon.*

Crystal Y. Dixon (Ohio, US)

A Lesson in Giving

Read 2 Corinthians 9:6–15

Like good stewards of the manifold grace of God, serve one another with whatever gift each of you has received.

1 Peter 4:10 (NRSV)

To me there is something special about belonging to a church in a small town. We know not only our church family, but also almost everyone else in town and how they are doing. Over the years, our church has worked to collect food, clothing and money for those who have fallen on hard times—whether they are members of our church or not.

Finally, the economic downturn affecting everyone else began affecting our church too. Our giving to others slowly but steadily grew less and less frequent. By the end of the year, we were giving nothing at all.

Then, on the first Sunday of the new year, our pastor preached on the importance of caring for one another, reminding us that even though Jesus was not rich in money, he used other gifts to help those in need. That day our congregation decided that we too would use the gifts we had to help the needy in our town.

Our gifts may not have been the biggest in terms of money, but we took a step in the right direction. All of us, givers and recipients alike, learned that even when our pockets are empty, God's love keeps us rich in our hearts.

Prayer: *Dear Lord, help us always to remember that when life is difficult, we have your light to show us the way. Amen*

Thought for the day: Generosity is a matter of attitude not amount.

Mark A. Carter (Texas, US)

Which are You?

Read Romans 5:1–10

Bless the Lord, O my soul, and do not forget all his benefits.
Psalm 103:2 (NRSV)

We can easily praise God when we feel blessed and things are going well. However, can we still praise God if we face difficulties? Can we keep our faith if we do not sense God's help?

These questions reminded me of an illustration. If carrots, eggs and coffee beans are boiled, the effect on each item will be different. The carrots will soften, the eggs will harden, and the coffee beans will change the colour of the water and spread a delicious aroma. The boiling water symbolises problems or pressures in our life. The carrots, eggs, and coffee beans symbolise different human reactions to problems or pressures. The soft carrots represent people who grumble, complain and pity themselves when faced with problems. The hardened eggs represent those who become stubborn, rebellious and angry with God during tribulations. But the coffee beans represent people who obey and trust God, changing the atmosphere around them while spreading the fragrance of Christ.

God offers to each of us faith greater than any problem we face. The magnitude of the problem is not as important as our reaction to the problem. Our faith determines how we will respond as we meet the challenges of daily life—as a carrot, a hard-boiled egg or a coffee bean.

Prayer: *Dear God of comfort, give us grateful hearts as we face our problems. Whatever the challenge, let us praise you always. Amen*

Thought for the day: When God's people find themselves in hot water, they can still be witnesses to grace.

Marcelina Dewi Kumalasari (Jakarta, Indonesia)

 PRAYER FOCUS: SOMEONE FACING A TROUBLING SITUATION

Not Junk

Read Luke 15:1–10

Suppose a woman has ten silver coins and loses one. Does she not light a lamp, sweep the house and search carefully until she finds it? And when she finds it, she calls her friends and neighbours together and says, 'Rejoice with me.'

Luke 15:8–9 (NIV)

My five-year-old daughter lost an earring in the car. When I cleaned the car, I sucked the earring into my vacuum. Then I disassembled the vacuum and began to search. I hadn't emptied my vacuum cleaner in months; but after an hour of sifting through gum wrappers, dirt, pet hair, and dried up bits of food, I found the earring. I entered the house expecting a hero's welcome, but my daughter was not especially joyful. She had already forgotten about the earring. My efforts—the time I had spent and the junk I had waded through to recover this forgotten, nearly-worthless earring—were not met with joy and thankfulness.

As I thought about my daughter's response, I began to wonder how God feels about our response to salvation. God has waded through piles of earthly junk for us, and God's search cost the life of Jesus. While we may feel nearly worthless and forgettable, clearly God's desire is to seek and save us. God desires to be reconciled and forever connected to us. While we may not understand what God has done, in Christ God saves us. And that is reason for joy!

Prayer: *Praise God, who searches for us, finds us and brings us home in Jesus Christ. Amen*

Thought for the day: The gift of salvation calls for joy and thanksgiving.

Robert Ames (Colorado, US)

Get it Right

Read Colossians 3:1–11

I am confident of this, that the one who began a good work among you will bring it to completion by the day of Jesus Christ.

Philippians 1:6 (NRSV)

I routinely have lunch with a group of colleagues. One of them is passionate about the art of origami. He takes small pieces of paper, folds them carefully, and creates various figures. If the figures aren't quite right, he takes them apart, consults the instruction manual and starts again until the figure is perfect.

When another member of the group tried to reproduce an origami figure and couldn't quite master it, he gave up. The advice of our friend was to be patient, to persevere, to consult the manual or simply to ask for help.

Thinking about this experience, I see a connection with the journey of Christians. When we began our faith journey, God's grace was already at work. Spiritual development is a process, and we encounter difficulties and obstacles along the way. So we persevere with patience. We study the Bible, our instruction manual, learn from other believers and ask God's help through prayer. All along the way, God watches over us and helps us in the journey.

Prayer: *God of hope, help us travel our road with faith and confidence in you. Save us from giving up or detouring from your path. Amen*

Thought for the day: Wherever we are in our journey, God helps us to move ahead.

Maria M. Urdaz (Puerto Rico)

Second Chances

Read Luke 15:11–32

Be kind and compassionate to one another, forgiving each other, just as in Christ God forgave you.

Ephesians 4:32 (NIV)

The prodigal son left home and wasted his money in wild living while his older brother stayed at home and behaved well. Then, when hard times came, the prodigal returned home and his father welcomed him as if he were a prince.

Until recently, I viewed this story through the eyes of the angry older brother. Why would the father reward bad behaviour and freely forgive the younger son? Then I experienced having a prodigal in my own family. Seeing that lost one return and change former destructive behaviour brought great joy. I could gladly forgive and celebrate.

Now I see the message of God's grace in the prodigal son's story. Like the father, God forgives and loves us, rejoicing when we come home. God's grace is free. Not one of us deserves it. Not one of us can earn it. We can only rejoice in the complete joy of second chances and our Father's awesome love.

Prayer: *O Lord, help us have forgiving hearts. May we love as you love—without judging and condemning. Amen*

Thought for the day: God loves us more than we can imagine.

Phyllis Stone Church (Kentucky, US)

Endless Wonder

Read Psalm 119:33–40

O the depth of the riches and wisdom and knowledge of God!

Romans 11:33 (NRSV)

My friend was concerned about the plight of homeless people in his neighbourhood. He helped them with money and food. But one day a homeless person challenged him that he really did not understand what it means to be homeless. So my friend decided to live at a homeless shelter for a week. It was a life-changing experience for him. He said, 'In the past, I knew about people's pains from a distance. Now I know their pain in my bones.'

Willingness to learn and to change, as my friend did, is also essential in developing our relationship with God. Christians may suffer from spiritual apathy, thinking we know enough about God. King David displayed a better spirit. David was called 'a man after [God's] own heart' (see 1 Samuel 13:13–14 and Acts 13:21–22). David looked honestly at himself and asked God to help him change. Surely this was a part of his pleasing God. This is reflected in Psalm 51:10: 'Create in me a clean heart, O God, and put a new and right spirit within me.'

Each day we can be willing to learn about the people we encounter, especially looking to see how God is working in and around us. When we do, we will learn that there is much goodness and majesty yet to be discovered—in God and in those around us.

Prayer: *Majestic God, help us to learn about you and your people so we may be compassionate and ready to help people. Amen*

Thought for the day: We can always learn more about God and his ways.

Keith Andrew Hwang (California, US)

Even Peter

Read John 21:15–19

[The shepherd] calls his own sheep by name and leads them out.

John 10:3 (NIV)

'The Lord loved even Peter.' These words, spoken by our pastor of my youth, woke me out of my normal Sunday evening stupor. I attended church three times each Sunday, and this was evening—the time when my thoughts wandered easily. Why did the Lord love even Peter? The preacher was describing how Peter had denied Jesus three times, but how there, by the Sea of Galilee, Peter was brought into the full love of the risen Christ (see John 21).

The pastor had emphasised his point, and now I was wide awake. He loves even Peter? That must mean me! I could feel tears filling my eyes. I was 14, and 14-year-old boys don't cry. My mother noticed the tears and asked me if I was all right. I just simply said, 'I've given my life to Jesus.' She hugged me and said, 'That's wonderful! What's happened?' I replied, 'Because Jesus loved even Peter, so he loves me.'

Christ the Good Shepherd knows his own sheep by name. When Christ called to Mary at the tomb, she recognised the Lord and told others that he was alive. Isn't it amazing that Christ knows each one of us by name? And if we listen, we will hear him call and we can follow him—not only to be loved but also to love. Your name may not be Peter, but the Lord loves even you.

Prayer: *Dear Lord, we thank you that you know each of us by name. Help us to hear you calling so that we can respond to your love and in your power love others. Amen*

Thought for the day: Today, Christ is calling my name.

Peter Whatton (Devon, England)

Too Small for God?

Read Ezekiel 40:1–14

All scripture is inspired by God and is useful for teaching, for reproof, for correction, and for training in righteousness.
2 Timothy 3:16 (NRSV)

I make it a habit to read through the Bible every year. I love the sense of familiarity with the whole Bible this practice gives me. However, I confess I don't love every part of the Bible equally. Encountering a passage like Ezekiel's trip to measure the temple (Ezekiel 40—42), I read quickly. My brain is not comfortable with long lists of measurements and compass directions; I don't come away with a clear mental picture of the story.

Nevertheless, even in the passages I find boring I look for something to apply in my life. After reading through books like Ezekiel, I tell myself repeatedly that God obviously pays great attention to details. This comforts me because 'the devil is in the details' quite often in my life. I wonder how schedules are going to work, how I'll be able to accomplish tasks in time or how I'll clean up the mess from trouble caused by some detail I overlooked.

Despite the Bible's reminders of divine attention to detail, I still wonder if I should pester God with prayers about tiny daily concerns. Yesterday, with my head still reeling from trying to understand cubits and pillars, I heard a clear answer: can I have a prayer request too small for the God who planned and measured and recorded all these things?

Prayer: *Thank you, God, for paying attention to the details of our lives. Help us always to expect to learn something from your word. Amen*

Thought for the day: The God who numbers my hairs can also order my days (see Matthew 10:30).

Jennifer Aaron (Washington, US)

No Words

Read 2 Corinthians 1:3–5

Rejoice with those who rejoice, weep with those who weep.

Romans 12:15 (NRSV)

One of my wife's close friends was upset over what was happening to her beloved husband. When she telephoned, my wife simply listened and encouraged her to remember that God would see her through.

Just after my father died, my father-in-law (or 'father-in-love' as I like to refer to him) met me at my house and simply held me in his big arms for a long time until my tears began to subside. What a blessing that was! We need friends to be with us in our suffering, standing with us, offering not advice or opinion but simply love and care.

Scripture speaks powerfully of God empathising with us: 'In all their distress [God] too was distressed... In his love and mercy he redeemed them; he lifted them up and carried them' (Isaiah 63:9, NIV). 'The Spirit helps us in our weakness... that very Spirit intercedes with sighs too deep for words' (Romans 8:26, NRSV). We embody this God when we stand with those in pain.

Prayer: *O God, help me this day to love and care for those you have put in my life. Amen*

Thought for the day: Those in pain need our presence more often than they need any words.

James A. Brunner (Arizona, US)

A Labour of Love

Read 1 Corinthians 12:1–11

Every good and perfect gift is from above, coming down from the Father of the heavenly lights, who does not change like shifting shadows.
James 1:17 (NIV)

The basement of my mother's block of flats seems an unlikely place to hang a portrait of a lovely young woman. Yet that's where it is. Wearing a ruffled dress, a straw hat and holding flowers, she seems to watch over residents hurrying in and out. Her identity is a mystery because the painting bears no title or signature. I wonder how many people notice this beautiful artwork hidden in such an unlikely place.

I realised the same could be said about many Christians. Some are 'hidden' on the mission field. Others are hidden in office cubicles, at home rearing children, working in nursing homes or some other place where they are not often noticed. The places and situations are as varied as the human race. God has given every believer at least one talent or spiritual gift to use. The artist who created the painting did this, making part of the world more beautiful. By using our talents and gifts, we do the same. But more than that, we reflect God's character and love. Each kind word, helpful deed and act of obedience proclaims God's grace.

Prayer: *Dear God, fill us with your Holy Spirit and guide our efforts so that all we say and do brings glory to you. Amen*

Thought for the day: How am I reflecting God's love today?

Flora Reigada (Florida, US)

Riding in the Slipstream

Read Hebrews 10:23–25

Where two or three are gathered together in my name, there am I in the midst of them.

Matthew 18:20 (KJV)

Cycling is a team sport. A cycler who rides in the slipstream of another can exert up to 30 per cent less effort and thus can save energy for the climax of the race. Even recreational cyclers enjoy the benefit of riding in a 'pace line'. In these, riders alternate riding in front. The lead rider endures the wind resistance, making riding easier for those who follow.

Life with its chaos, challenges, confusion, anxiety and weariness is like cycling into a fierce headwind. We all know moments when things are going well, as if we were being pulled along without much effort, as if we were at the back or in the middle of a pace line. But we are also familiar with times of struggle, weariness and loneliness that push us to our limit. It's like fighting a headwind. But as the writer of Hebrews admonishes, we can meet and work together to support and help one another in our struggles. When we do, Christ is there with us, helping to pull us along!

Prayer: *All-powerful God, thank you for helping us through the difficult times in our lives. Remind us to look for others who are struggling and to lend them comfort and support. Amen*

Thought for the day: Each day, look for someone who needs your help—and give it in the name of Christ.

Charles T. Beemer (Dominican Republic)

Prayer Workshop

The Problem of Pain

Suffering is inevitable. We don't like to hear that, but it's true. I once heard a speaker say, 'In this life, misery is optional. Suffering is not, but misery is.' Those words call us to face and admit the reality of suffering. And they remind us that we have some power over the way we respond when suffering comes. As much as we would like to believe that we can avoid hurt, struggle and loss, life brings difficulties to all of us. For some, these difficulties threaten their faith. Some people say that God cannot be good and also allow the evil and suffering that are part of this world. For some, life's pain becomes so overwhelming that they write God off as unconcerned or they turn away from believing.

Human nature wants to avoid pain. We want ourselves and those we care about to be spared from it. We see an illustration of this in the Gospel of Matthew, when Jesus tells the disciples that he 'must go to Jerusalem and undergo great suffering' (Matthew 16:21, NRSV). Peter takes Jesus aside and begins 'to rebuke him, saying, "God forbid it, Lord"' (Matthew 16:22). Peter doesn't want Jesus to suffer because he loves him. We are all somewhat like Peter when it comes to those we love.

When suffering comes, questions are natural: does God want us to suffer? Does God allow the pain we endure? Does God even, as some say, send suffering to 'teach us a lesson', to 'bring us to our knees'? The Bible tells us in many places that the answer to those questions is no. God wants shalom—peace, well-being, redemption and healing—for us and for the world. Jesus said, 'I came that they may have life, and have it abundantly' (John 10:10).

In Jesus' life and works we see clearly what God wants for us: that we live in close friendship with God and in healing relationships with one another. God is completely good and desires only good for us. But we live in a fallen world, with fallen and fallible people, and so pain comes to all of us. Suffering causes us to admit that we are not all-powerful, that we cannot control life and insulate ourselves and others from pain. Still, in the Bible passage referred to above, we see Jesus continuing toward Jerusalem after that encounter with Peter, healing people even as he walked a road that he knew led to suffering. Jesus showed us that some suffering can be redemptive.

So how will we deal with suffering? Hard times can make us bitter, or they can make us better. Hard times can elicit from us strength and patience and courage that we did not know we had. Many years ago, one of my nieces died after being hit by a truck while out riding her bicycle. As I watched my brother deal with the other children and with his broken-hearted wife during the days that followed, I was amazed by his patience, strength and tenderness. Tragic circumstances brought out the best in him; he was more than I had known him to be.

Suffering can harden our hearts, but it can also make our hearts more tender toward others in their times of pain and loss. The first chapter of 2 Corinthians tells us that God, the 'God of all comfort', consoles us in our affliction so that we may be able to console others (vv. 3–4, KJV). Suffering can shape us to be more like Christ, to be a healing presence.

We can also shape our suffering. We can transform it, even as it challenges us. Many people turn their pain into energy for redemptive purposes. A couple in my church has begun speaking to teenagers about the dangers of distracted driving. Their son was killed when someone talking on a mobile phone crossed the white line and collided head-on with his car. The man who founded Make Today Count and helped thousands who face terminal illnesses did so after his own diagnosis of cancer. Walter Everett, a clergyman whose son was killed, befriended the young man who murdered his son and became an example of amazing forgiveness. These people shaped their suffering. Stories like theirs remind us of the power of the human spirit and of God's power to help us live through and move beyond life's wounds and losses. They remind us that when pain comes, God offers us comfort and—as our season of grieving passes—hope and healing.

Several meditations in this issue touch on the subject of suffering. These writers invite us to remember that just as God was with Jesus during his suffering and resurrection, so God is with us in the midst of our pain, offering resurrection and the hope of new beginnings. You may want to read the meditations and suggested scripture passages for May 1, 8 and 17, June 6 and 28, July 6, 10, 12, 22, 23, 26, 28 and 30, and August 2, 5, 7, 10, 14, 19 and 28 before answering the reflection questions below.

Questions for Reflection:

1. Recall a recent news story about a tragedy or loss. Were there related reports that offered hope as well as information about the tragedy? How did you respond inwardly and outwardly to the reports?

2. Jeremiah 29:11 says, 'I know the plans I have for you, says the Lord, plans for your welfare... to give you a future with hope.' Where in your life do you need to hear this word from God at the moment? How can you reach out to someone you know who needs to hear this message?

3. Thinking back over your life, consider some difficult experience that taught you something about caring for people. What was the experience, and what did you learn?

4. What questions would you like to ask God about suffering?

5. What are the gifts in suffering? How can we look for the positives in our difficult and traumatic experiences? How has God come to you in those times?

6. What passage(s) or stories from scripture challenge you when you think about suffering or loss? Which ones offer you guidance and comfort in difficult times?

Mary Lou Redding

Food for the Soul

Read John 6:1–13

When they were satisfied, [Jesus] told his disciples, 'Gather up the fragments left over, so that nothing may be lost.'

John 6:12 (NRSV)

Scripture does not tell us how the surplus food was dispersed after Jesus fed the multitude. However, we can be sure that the extra morsels were not thrown away. The Lord said, 'Gather up the fragments left over, so that nothing may be lost.'

Jesus' statement raises several questions. Was the food saved for the disciples? Did the disciples carry the baskets with them as they continued their journey? Was the leftover bread distributed to the poor? Whatever the case, the food was not wasted.

Our church has a long tradition of working to meet people's basic needs. Each Sunday we collect non-perishable items for distribution at a hostel for the homeless. We donate leftovers from our church dinners to an organisation that operates from our church taking meals to the elderly or housebound. We try to follow Christ's message, to gather up extra food so that nothing is lost.

Although our efforts are minuscule compared to the world's need, we can help to alleviate the hunger of our near neighbours. Whether feeding five thousand, five hundred or five, we can follow Christ's example of providing food to the hungry.

Prayer: *Dear God, guide us to meet people's needs for food, companionship and compassion. May we follow Christ's example by extending a hand to those in need. Amen*

Thought for the day: Giving food for the body opens the door to sharing food for the soul.

Link2Life: *Can you set up a food distribution service from your church?*

Fritzie Meier (Pennsylvania, US)

Letters from My Father

Read Psalm 19:7–11

Lay hold of my words with all your heart.
Proverbs 4:4 (NIV)

During my teenage years, my father wrote many letters to me. At the time I thought little of them. I knew he meant well, but another long letter about how proud he was of me and how God's favour was on my life seemed overdone at times. But after my father's death in a car accident, I started cherishing those letters.

After reading Proverbs 4:4, I realised that my heavenly Father was trying to get my attention. I had been reading God's word in the way I used to read my father's letters—with apathy and disinterest. But God revealed to me that I could benefit from the Bible's wisdom if I read intending to learn and apply God's truth to my life.

Just as my earthly father left me letters of motivation and encouraged me to stay close to God, my heavenly Father has given me the Bible and its guidance for my life (Jeremiah 29:11). The Bible constantly reminds me how much God loves me (John 3:16), and it is there to keep me on the path to a blessed life.

Prayer: *Dear Lord, thank you for your word that guides us to a fulfilling life. Help us to take the time to learn your ways. Make your word our heart's desire so that we can live in obedience to you. As Jesus taught us, we pray, 'Father, hallowed be your name, your kingdom come. Give us each day our daily bread. Forgive us our sins, for we also forgive everyone who sins against us. And lead us not into temptation.'* *

Thought for the day: How can I make more space in my heart for God?

Melanie Leo (Cape Town, South Africa)

 PRAYER FOCUS: BIBLE STUDY GROUPS

* Luke 11:2–4 (NIV)

Behold the Beautiful

Read 1 Samuel 16:1–7

The Lord said to Samuel, 'Do not consider his appearance or his height, for I have rejected him. The Lord does not look at the things man looks at. Man looks at the outward appearance, but the Lord looks at the heart.'

1 Samuel 16:7 (NIV)

During renovation of our nearly-200-year-old house, the construction workers covered one unfinished wall with a blue plastic tarpaulin to keep out draughts and to keep down the dust. When my four-year-old grandson saw it, he exclaimed, 'Oh, Granny! That's beautiful!' I had to laugh. What seemed unattractive to us adults he perceived as beautiful.

I think that God must see each of us as my grandson saw the tarpaulin. When we see someone we may focus only on their haircut or clothes or jewellery. We may judge them to be anything from rich and successful to down-and-out. We may judge ourselves the same way, feeling acceptable or unacceptable based simply on how we look.

But God looks on the inside and sees who we truly are and how valuable each of us is. As we serve God and others, we become inwardly and lastingly beautiful.

Prayer: *Loving God, thank you for accepting and loving us just as we are. Help us to grow more and more like Christ. In Jesus' name. Amen*

Thought for the day: God loves and accepts us regardless of our outer appearance.

Sandra Vaughan (Pennsylvania, US)

PRAYER FOCUS: CONSTRUCTION WORKERS

Prophet of Hope

Read Isaiah 61:1–4

The spirit of the Lord God is upon me, because the Lord has anointed me; he has sent me to bring good news to the oppressed, to bind up the broken hearted, to proclaim liberty to the captives, and release to the prisoners.

Isaiah 61:1 (NRSV)

As a teenager, I stood awestruck at the Statue of Liberty. In the shadow of Ellis Island, where so many had arrived in a new land, the United States, full of possibility and hope, I read the poem by Emma Lazarus 'The New Colossus'. Its words about welcoming 'the homeless, tempest-tost' opened my eyes.

Somehow, living in the relative comfort and privilege of my rural home, I had not learned that others were not as comfortable and privileged as I. As I read the poem, I began to understand that the statue was a symbol of welcome for those who are not like me. Eventually, I came to realise that beyond national allegiance our faith calls us to welcome the stranger, to care for the homeless, to give hope to the dreamer, to offer a place of possibility to those who seek a better life.

At the core of scripture is a message of compassion for the poor and the oppressed and passion for mercy and justice. God's way is to seek freedom from oppression; 'to do justice, and to love kindness, and to walk humbly with your God' (Micah 6:8) so that the possibilities of hope may be accomplished and available to all.

Prayer: *Dear God, show us what we need to do to live for your purposes. Amen*

Thought for the day: How do we welcome the needy?

F. Richard Garland (New Hampshire, US)

 PRAYER FOCUS: TO FOLLOW GOD'S CALL

Looking Ahead

Read Proverbs 4:20–27

Let your eyes look directly forwards, and your gaze be straight before you.
Proverbs 4:25 (NRSV)

When I was a small boy, I wanted to learn to ride a bicycle. One of the happiest days of my life was when my older brother said he would teach me, using his bicycle. But I was shorter than he was, and my feet did not reach the bike's pedals when they were at the bottom. Finally, I managed to get out on the street, where my brother told me to always look ahead, not down at my feet. But I spent much of my time looking down, trying to keep my feet on the pedals. Not long after I began my ride, I tumbled into a roadside vendor, knocking her over and spilling her basket of water nuts. I learned the value of looking ahead!

Looking ahead is important also in our spiritual life. We can easily get stuck focusing on our inabilities, hindrances and shortcomings both in our work and our personal lives. But the writer of Proverbs shows us the way out: 'Let your eyes look directly forward.' Many times as I have lifted my head and focused on the Lord in prayer, I have been able to move on through the rugged times in my life.

I finally learned to ride a bicycle simply by looking ahead and knowing that the pedals would come up on their own to reach my feet. In the spiritual life we can do the same, trusting that what we need will come in time as we keep looking ahead, following Christ who leads us.

Prayer: *Dear Lord, help us to focus on your way as we make our spiritual journey. Do not allow us to fall on the roadside. Keep us alert, always with our eyes looking forward. Amen*

Thought for the day: Our focus determines whether we are moving closer to God or further away.

Claudius Kashi Tewari (Uttar Pradesh, India)

In Hard Places

Read James 1:2–4

We are hard pressed on every side, but not crushed; perplexed, but not in despair.

2 Corinthians 4:8 (NIV)

Pain: we all experience it. Pain often leaves a mark on our lives, a permanent scar on our hearts. At two months old, our daughter Sarah was diagnosed with a life-threatening liver disease. This illness began an emotionally exhausting time for our family. At one point, she lost almost all the blood in her body; my wife and I feared we would lose her. But we didn't. God blessed her with the gift of a new liver in April 2009. Sarah's illness and transplant surgery strained our family.

Yet we were never far from God's care and grace. We found God in the many friends who stayed with us in the hospital. We found God in the body of Christ, believers we know and those around the world we did not know, who were praying for our family. We found God in the personal care our church provided. We saw God in the way money came in to pay for what we needed.

We still live day to day, praying that Sarah's transplanted liver will not fail and that she can live a long and happy life. At the end of the day, her life is in God's hands. God's faithfulness allows us to live at all, now and for eternity.

Prayer: *Dear Lord, remind us you are with us no matter what paths we must walk. Amen*

Thought for the day: In the midst of pain, tremendous blessings can bloom.

Kirk Kraft (Washington, US)

 PRAYER FOCUS: THOSE AWAITING ORGAN TRANSPLANTS

God's Stain Remover

Read 1 John 1:5–9

If we confess our sins, he who is faithful and just will forgive us our sins and cleanse us from all unrighteousness.

1 John 1:9 (NRSV)

While sitting on the train, I pondered the day's events. Especially heavy on my mind was an angry comment I had made to a colleague. Not wanting to think about it, I turned to talk to a man who was blind. Soon he asked, 'Someone said that I have a stain on my jacket, but I can't feel a wet spot. Would you mind telling me if there really is a stain?' Unfortunately, I had to confirm that there was a large, dried stain on the front of his coat.

Later I thought about how those two events intertwined. My rudeness at work was a type of inward stain that I could not touch or see—a stain of offence against my colleague.

I decided to open up my heart in prayer and ask God to forgive and cleanse me. I also apologised to my colleague, who graciously forgave me. A wonderful, warm feeling spread over me, as if I were stepping out into bright sunlight after a long, grey winter. I knew I had truly been forgiven. A blind man taught me to see.

Prayer: *Source of our light, bless us with the forgiveness that brings us freedom from offences. In Jesus' name we pray. Amen*

Thought for the day: God's love can remove even the toughest inner stain.

Janet L. Williams (Missouri, US)

The Key to Peace

Read Luke 15:1–7

As a father has compassion for his children, so the Lord has compassion for those who fear him.

Psalm 103:13 (NRSV)

One night while we were getting ready for bed, my eight-year-old daughter told me her teacher had said that she loves all 44 children in her class equally and that her students were like her own children. Excited by her teacher's words, my daughter kept saying that her teacher was special and that she could go to her if she had any problem at school.

Seeing her happiness and confidence in her teacher's love, I realised how much more we can be at peace in God's presence. God loves all of us equally. God knows when we are in trouble and will take extra care of those who need special attention. When a lost child is found, God's joy has no bounds. God is like a loving father who faithfully watches over his beloved children.

Remembering that is our key to peace. Life can be a fulfilling journey when we trust God with both our joys and sorrows. Our joys are multiplied and our sorrows diminished when we know that God is with us.

Prayer: *Dear Father, thank you for being with us in joy and sorrow, at work and at leisure, during times of pain and times of ease. Thank you for providing solutions to the problems we face. Amen*

Thought for the day: Knowing God diminishes our sorrows and multiplies our joys.

Elizabeth Alex Thomas (Al 'Asimah, Kuwait)

Just a Mosquito?

Read Romans 16:1–16

Give my greetings to the brothers at Laodicea, and to Nympha and the church in her house.

Colossians 4:15 (NRSV)

I love reading over the lists of names at the end of Paul's letters. I imagine who the people were, what they were like, and what roles they played in the earliest days of the Christian movement. I'm intrigued that most of them are obscure and yet profoundly important—actually, like most of us. However, none of us is too obscure to make a contribution. As the saying goes, 'If you think you are too small to make a difference, try spending the night in a closed room with a mosquito.'

Most likely, you and I will never be famous. But by living in faithful obedience to Jesus, offering ourselves to God, we can make an eternal difference. We're all much like that little boy who gave his loaves and fishes to Jesus: we don't have a lot in our hands, but in the hands of the Son of God, what we give can feed a multitude.

Prayer: *O God, we give thanks for all the obscure people who built the Church and kept the faith alive for us. Help us to be as faithful as they were so that all those around us may come into relationship with you. Amen*

Thought for the day: No matter how unimportant I feel, I matter as a servant of God.

Dan G. Johnson (Florida, US)

PRAYER FOCUS: UNAPPRECIATED SERVANTS OF GOD

Every Day Is Christmas

Read Luke 2:1–11

I am bringing you good news of great joy for all the people: to you is born this day in the city of David a Saviour, who is the Messiah, the Lord.
Luke 2:10–11 (NRSV)

Every time I visit Martha at the nursing home, she asks, 'Are you getting ready for Christmas?' Dementia makes her unaware of the actual date. This reality does not trouble Martha, and over the years it has ceased to trouble me.

Some have said, 'Correct her. Help her to understand that Christmas is months away.' For a long time, I attempted to do this, but now I see the value of expecting the birth of Jesus every day. I watch Martha's face light up with joy when she asks, 'Are you getting ready for Christmas?' Her eyes dance and her smile changes the mood in the room. She expects Christmas to come and for Jesus to be born today or maybe tomorrow—very soon. And this brings her joy that is contagious.

In the midst of all that could attempt to defeat the message of Christmas, Martha reminds all of us around her that Jesus is coming. Jesus is coming soon. Her simple question has changed me. I now leave a nativity set on a table in my office throughout the year to help me remember the truth, 'To you is born a Saviour.' I give thanks for the gift of Martha's question and for its reminder to expect Jesus to come—today and every day.

Prayer: *In the bustle of our lives, help us, O God, to remember that you come to us each day—whether it's Christmas time or not. Amen*

Thought for the day: Every day we can find signs of Christ's presence.

Karen Greenwaldt (Tennessee, US)

 PRAYER FOCUS: TO ANTICIPATE JESUS' COMING EVERY DAY

In God's Hands

Read Psalm 31:1–8

I am the Lord your God who takes hold of your right hand and says to you, Do not fear; I will help you.

Isaiah 41:13 (NIV)

One of the lessons we teach our young children is to hold the hand of an adult when crossing the road so they will be safe. But my teenage grandsons still like to hold their grandma's hand as a sign of affection and care. They hold the hands of their girlfriends out of love. Throughout our lives, we trust the hands of others as we experience care and comfort and are held in love.

In a spiritual sense, we are invited to place ourselves in the hands of God, our protector, just as Jesus did when on the cross (see Luke 23:46). We do not know what lies ahead for any of us. Our paths may take frightening detours or turns. We may feel as though we are being pursued by enemies. Sometimes we go down to the pit of despair with feelings of fear and doubt. We need someone to hold us during our difficult time.

Whether we are just beginning life or nearing the end of it, we are invited to trust God to guide us and protect us. We give thanks for the many loving hands that hold us—those of parents, grandparents, friends and spouses. But by far the best hands that hold us are the hands of God. These hands that form us hold us in faithful and steadfast love.

Prayer: *Dear God, thank you for all who lift us up and support us. Remind us to rely on you above all others. Amen*

Thought for the day: 'If God is for us, who can be against us?' (Romans 8:31).

Sandi Marr (Ontario, Canada)

The Strawberry Plant

Read Psalm 37:23–31

'Be still, and know that I am God! I am exalted among the nations, I am exalted in the earth.'

Psalm 46:10 (NRSV)

Early in the spring while working in my garden, I noticed a strawberry plant that had not been there before. I was puzzled and wondered where it had come from; I had not planted it. Then I remembered that a year earlier I had bought a kit containing a strawberry pot, some compost and some strawberry seeds. I had planted the seeds in the pot, put it in a sunny spot on my patio, and watered it throughout the spring and summer. The seeds barely sprouted; so in the autumn, feeling discouraged, I threw the dried-up contents of the pot into a corner of my garden. A year later, I found a strawberry plant flourishing there.

Seeing that strawberry plant has encouraged me. Many times when I face frustration, despair and fear, I feel hopeless and want to just give up. Now when I see the strawberry plant in my garden, I remember that God is always at work, no matter how bleak my circumstances and no matter what I am facing. God provides us with hope and encouragement to help us deal with life's challenges.

Prayer: *Dear God, when we are discouraged and ready to give up, remind us that you will never leave us or forsake us. Amen*

Thought for the day: Even when I am overwhelmed, God is not.

Elizabeth A. Methe (Massachusetts, US)

Context

Read Galatians 6:7–11

Paul wrote, 'Let us work for the good of all.'

Galatians 6:10 (NRSV)

Context is everything; knowing the context in which someone said something keeps the words from becoming tools of destruction. Knowing the context of a beloved, often-quoted saying may enrich its meaning even more. Like many people, I grew up hearing snippets of the Bible all the time. I heard some phrases or sayings from the Bible outside of organised religion. Even though context is important, tone can carry equal weight. I remember as a child hearing Paul's words to the Galatians, 'Do not be deceived; God is not mocked, for you reap whatever you sow.' I often heard these words as chiding and chastising. I received them as a negative warning.

While Paul discourages believers in Galatia from 'sowing to the flesh', he presents a balanced picture, reminding them that in sowing to the Spirit that 'will reap eternal life from the Spirit'. Paul's words build to a great crescendo of encouragement: 'So let us not grow weary in doing what is right, for we will reap at harvest-time, if we do not give up.'

These are not the words of someone shaking a finger in another's face as if expecting him or her to do the wrong thing. These are words of encouragement, cheering us on as we persist in doing the right thing.

Prayer: *Dear God, help us know your word and proclaim it. By the power of your word, give us life. Amen*

Thought for the Day: God wants to help us make the right choices.

Gregory V. Palmer (Ohio, US)

PRAYER FOCUS: SOMEONE MAKING A DIFFICULT DECISION

Our Greatest Wealth

Read Matthew 6:19–24

You cannot serve both God and Money.

Matthew 6:24 (NIV)

When I was nine or ten years old, I worked very hard at school. One Saturday morning I went with my father to buy a folder for a paper I had written for a homework assignment.

At the shop we found the shelf that displayed folders of many colours. I had to choose one of them. I looked at my father and said in a dreamy voice, 'Can you imagine how good it would be to have enough money to buy a folder of each colour?' My father wisely responded, 'But a school report card with the good grades you have—no money can buy that.'

At that moment his words touched me deeply, and I was quiet. I remember even today the smile on his face as he spoke. I believe my father's words were a part of a true Christian education. God's gifts and grace are to be valued more than the material goods we use.

Because many of us live in a consumer-oriented world, we sometimes tend to value what we can have over who we can be. But who we are through the gifts we receive from God is our greatest wealth.

Prayer: *Dear God, continue to inspire us to express and to live according to your values. Show us how to become all you dream us to be. In Jesus' name. Amen*

Thought for the day: Our identity as God's children is a greater asset than anything money can buy.

Norma Sarian (Sao Paulo, Brazil)

God Upholds Us

Read Psalm 63:3–8

My soul clings to you; your right hand upholds me.

Psalm 63:8 (NIV)

Each summer in Tennessee we are visited by hummingbirds migrating north from Central America. My wife and I watch these little creatures as they flutter and circle around our bird feeders, feeding on the nectar and also chasing each other. We marvel at their beauty, their tiny wings and their ability to hover in mid air.

One day after I heard a thud against the patio door, I saw a hummingbird on the ground. I picked it up and discovered that the small creature was stunned but still alive. For the next 15 minutes I held the little hummingbird in the palm of my hand. I stroked its feathers and talked gently to it until it regained its ability to fly. When I told my wife of my experience, she said it was like having the power of God in my hands.

I reflected on what my wife said and realised that what I did for the little bird is similar to the way God's hand upholds us. When we fall, God picks us up, holds us close and talks gently to us—helping us to regain our balance and to get our bearings. Holding the hummingbird in my hand was a magical moment but not nearly as awesome as the thought that our Lord does this every day for us.

Prayer: *Dear God, pick us up when we stumble and fall. Through your Holy Spirit, help us to find our way. Show us your will. Amen*

Thought for the day: No matter what today brings, I can trust God to hold me.

Gary Dowdy (Tennessee, US)

PRAYER FOCUS: CONSERVATIONISTS

Misplaced Hope

Read Matthew 19:16–22

Jesus answered [the rich young man], 'If you want to be perfect, go, sell your possessions and give to the poor, and you will have treasure in heaven. Then come, follow me.'

Matthew 19:21 (NIV)

For many years I believed that my job defined who I was. I placed my hope in the stability and security of the career I had chosen instead of in God. Then, as I was preparing to leave work one day, my supervisor called me into his office. He informed me that my position had been terminated, effective immediately. Fear flooded me as I realised that what I had put my hope in for the future was gone.

My situation reminded me of the story in Matthew 19 about a rich young man who also had misplaced hope. He had great wealth and was unwilling to let go of it and follow Jesus. But status, riches and possessions are empty substitutes for God. I now see that losing a job I thought was my hope for the future was the best thing that could have happened. During this upheaval in my life, I learned that God is faithful to meet all of my needs. Nothing this world offers can give me eternal hope; only God can do that.

Prayer: *Dear Father, you alone are our hope, today and for ever. Help us to trust you no matter what our circumstances. We pray as Jesus taught us, saying, 'Our Father in heaven, hallowed be your name, your kingdom come, your will be done on earth as it is in heaven. Give us today our daily bread. Forgive us our debts, as we also have forgiven our debtors. And lead us not into temptation, but deliver us from the evil one.'* Amen*

Thought for the day: Where am I placing my hope?

Noel McArtor (Nevada, US)

 PRAYER FOCUS: THOSE WHO FEEL HOPELESS

* Matthew 6:9–13 (NIV)

The Gift

Read Psalm 51:10–17

The sacrifice acceptable to God is a broken spirit; a broken and contrite heart, O God, you will not despise.

Psalm 51:17 (NRSV)

When my son was about two years old, he gave me a gift. It was a small pot that he had half filled with sand, into which he had stuck a single pink flower and a handful of leaves. The flower was faded and the leaves were withered; the pot itself was old, cracked and mud-crusted. But he presented it to me with eager hands, a sweet smile and a heart full of love. I accepted his gift with joy and placed it in a place of honour—at the very centre of my table.

Thinking about my son and his giving, I ask myself what I can offer God today. Do I offer distracted worship and stumbling words of praise? My inadequate thanks or insincere words of repentance? Myself, a flawed, sinful vessel? Flawed as they may be, I know that God accepts both me and my offerings with loving hands and a smile, delighting in my love and worship, simply because I am a beloved child.

Prayer: *Dear Lord, we are unworthy to stand before you. The best we have to offer seems too little. Yet you look beyond our offerings to the love in our hearts. Thank you for accepting our words of repentance, thanks and praise. Amen*

Thought for the day: God's love is a gift to us; our love for others is our gift to God.

Link2Life: *Think of an unexpected gift you can give to a loved one.*

Tanya Ferdinandusz (Western Province, Sri Lanka)

PRAYER FOCUS: THOSE WHO FEEL WORTHLESS

Seeking Good

Read Romans 12:9–18

Whoever diligently seeks good seeks favour, but evil comes to the one who searches for it.

Proverbs 11:27 (NRSV)

I sat in a coffee shop telling my friend how much I was dreading the imminent visit of one of my relatives. She listened, paused and then said, 'You know, if you're expecting him to annoy you, he will. You will find problems if you're looking for them.'

I sat in silence, digesting her words. Then I sighed and said, 'You're so right.' I knew I needed to change my attitude before my relative arrived.

Then I read Proverbs 11:27. The truth of how the verse applied to me was so clear that it startled me. Because I focused on the irritating behaviour of my relative, I could not appreciate him. He could be engaging, funny and pleasant. But up to this point I had missed out on all his good attributes because I wasn't looking for them. As the verse implies, we will find the negative if we look for it. Still, the opposite is also true. When we look for the good in people or situations, we really can find it.

My relative did come for a visit, and I was irritated at times. But I also enjoyed his humour, his generosity and his entertaining stories. And when he left, I thanked God for using my friend and scripture to show me that I was the one who needed to change.

Prayer: *Dear God, thank you for teaching us how to be more like you. Amen*

Thought for the day: Look more closely for the good!

Dana Ryan (California, US)

Late-day Worker

Read Matthew 20:1–16

[The landowner] replied to one of the [labourers], '... Am I not allowed to do what I choose with what belongs to me? Or are you envious because I am generous?'

Matthew 20:13-15 (NRSV)

I always struggled when I read the parable about the labourers in the vineyard. I empathised with the workers who felt they should earn more than those who worked part of the day because they worked the entire day. I have been a Christian since I was at primary school; I've shared the gospel by teaching Sunday school classes to people of various ages. I've helped out with holiday Bible clubs and volunteered with various mission works. Consequently, I thought I understood where those early-day workers were coming from. The landowner's behaviour seemed unfair to me, too.

But I changed my mind about those latecomers when my father-in-law, Albert, was dying of lung cancer. My husband and son talked with him often about God's love and mercy, and read to him their favourite Bible passages. We saw Albert change before our eyes. He wasn't healed from the cancer, but he became a changed person. And before he died, Albert helped to lead several others to Christ.

Albert was definitely a late-day worker, but he trusted in God's grace and received the same share as the rest of us. It may not seem fair, but it was right. Through Albert, my eyes and heart were opened to the true meaning in that parable, to see God's generous love for all of us.

Prayer: *O God, help us to appreciate your love, grace and mercy that we learn about through your work in the lives of others. Amen*

Thought for the day: The gift of salvation is the same, no matter when we come to Christ.

Donna Trimble (North Carolina, US)

Listener

Read Matthew 13:19–27

Let me hear what God the Lord will speak, for he will speak peace to his people, to his faithful, to those who turn to him in their hearts.
Psalm 85:8 (NRSV)

For some years I worked for a telephone crisis-counselling service. Each year, a new group of people was trained for this challenging and vital service. Part of the training involved listening exercises. In the time following this training, many trainees spoke of the difference it made in their lives. With awe and amazement, they told of the new depths they had found in relationships with family members, work colleagues, customers and even casual contacts.

Listening to other people is important, but how much more important it is to listen to what God is saying to us! Jesus said, 'Let anyone with ears listen!' (Matthew 13:9), but we forget that listening requires giving our attention. We hear God when we carefully attend to the Bible as we read it or hear it read. We hear God when we listen to the words of pastors, friends or fellow Christians. We hear God when we respond to particular thoughts emerging from the jumble in our minds. And we hear God when we respond to the pleas of the hungry, homeless or desperate.

Prayer: *All-powerful God, may we learn to listen with our heart, mind and will to your message of hope, encouragement and correction. Speak peace to our hearts each day. In Jesus' name. Amen*

Thought for the day: What is God saying to me today?

Everard Blackman (Queensland, Australia)

Sawing Sawdust

Read Philippians 4:4–9

Do not worry about anything, but in everything by prayer and supplication with thanksgiving let your requests be made known to God.

Philippians 4:6 (NRSV)

The phrase 'You can't saw sawdust!' means that we can't do anything about what is over and done with. But I think I've become proficient at sawing sawdust. From the time I wake up until I fall asleep, anxiety consumes me. No matter how hard I try, this irritant flutters in my restless mind. I feel concern for my responsibilities and relationships, as well as the future, the past, the present and events that are completely beyond my control. I've read many articles and book excerpts, studied many Bible verses, and prayed many, many times, but I hadn't changed in my compulsion to worry.

One day I started slowly to realise that my constant worry and anxiety only send a message to the Lord that I don't trust God's message sent through Paul: 'Do not worry about anything, but in everything by prayer and supplication with thanksgiving let your requests be made known to God' (Philippians 4:6). If I were able to do this, then the 'sawdust' I worry about can be replaced with peace.

Prayer: *Dear heavenly Father, help us to release the weight of our anxiety and fully trust you. Amen*

Thought for the day: Lasting peace comes from trusting God.

Bill Pike (Virginia, US)

PRAYER FOCUS: THOSE WHO WORRY CONTINUALLY

Love that Lasts

Read Romans 8:31–39

I am convinced that neither death nor life, neither angels nor demons, neither the present nor the future, nor any powers, neither height nor depth, nor anything else in all creation, will be able to separate us from the love of God that is in Christ Jesus our Lord.
Romans 8:38–39 (NIV)

My friend and his wife lost their only child, a daughter, in a car crash just over a year ago. Not knowing how to cope with the death of her daughter, my friend's wife began drinking excessively. Growing ever more bitter, she complained that everything her husband did bothered her. In response, he began to distance himself from her and went looking for affection from other women. Their marriage soon ended. While I was visiting my friend after the divorce was final, he sighed and said, 'Well, I guess love just wasn't meant to last for ever.'

Is my friend right? Will people always let us down and break our hearts? Can we ever find love that truly lasts?

I am grateful that the Bible says we can. God promises to love us always, no matter how life and other people treat us. In the death of our loved ones and even at the time of our own death, we can trust that God's love for us remains unchanged. In the midst of life's struggles, God's love carries us. Even though we don't know what will happen tomorrow, we can know that God will be waiting for us in love when we get there. God's love is truly love that lasts for ever.

Prayer: *Dear God, help us to be confident in your love today. Amen*

Thought for the day: Though people may fail us, God never will.

Link2Life: *Send a card to someone you know who is grieving.*

Stephen R. Wilson (Ohio, US)

The Colour of Betrayal

Read Colossians 3:12–17

Bear with each other and forgive whatever grievances you may have against one another. Forgive as the Lord forgave you.

Colossians 3:13 (NIV)

For years I did not like the colour purple. Purple was my best friend Jenny's favourite colour the year we were both eleven—the year Jenny betrayed me. Preferring more popular friends, Jenny made fun of me, abandoned me and even turned off lights to leave me alone in a dark room. In my mind, purple became the colour of disloyalty, painful feelings and memories I couldn't forgive. Or rather, memories I *wouldn't* forgive.

I didn't want to forgive. Jenny was wrong, and I was hurt. I held on to my bitter feelings until God showed me through scripture that we are to forgive others just as God forgives our sins. Compared to the ugliness of sin, even the most hideous shade of purple is beautiful.

If anyone had a right to feel bitter because of what people did to him, Jesus did. However, his response was amazing forgiveness. Judas betrayed Jesus to those who wanted him dead. Three times Peter denied knowing Jesus. Yet as Jesus, the sinless Son of God, died on the cross after the Roman guards scorned, mocked and beat him, he prayed, 'Father, forgive them…' (Luke 23:34).

Prayer: *Dear God, help us to follow Christ's example. Teach us to forgive others as you have forgiven us. In Jesus' name we pray. Amen*

Thought for the day: No hurt is too great for us to forgive.

Lochlanina Tobey (Virginia, US)

Because of the Cross

Read Jude 1:20–25

God made [Christ] who had no sin to be sin for us, so that in him we might become the righteousness of God.

2 Corinthians 5:21 (NIV)

Arriving at a friend's house, I was somewhat surprised to see a rugged, thick-beamed wooden cross in the yard. Then I realised that it had been erected to support the two big branches of a large yucca tree that was bending over too far. The cross beam, each side supporting a branch, was preventing the tree from leaning further over and uprooting. It was also encouraging the tree to grow upward.

'How symbolic this is of Jesus' death and victory on the cross for us!' I thought. His arms outstretched on the cross take the full weight of our sin, preventing us from toppling over to spiritual death and encouraging us to grow in our faith.

This yucca tree was saved, but its growth upwards will take some time. Isn't this how it is with us? We are saved by Jesus' death on the cross, but our growth takes time. The owner of the yucca saw the value of the tree, even though it was leaning over, and saved it instead of chopping it down. In a similar way, Jesus Christ sees the value in each of us even when we are 'leaned over'. With amazing love, Christ saves us. Great is God's joy as we flourish, growing stronger day by day.

Prayer: *Dear Jesus, thank you for your grace that saves us. Help us to heed your Holy Spirit so that we may grow to become more and more like you. Amen*

Thought for the day: Salvation is only the beginning of what God wants to do in us.

Elaine Richardson (Western Cape, South Africa)

 PRAYER FOCUS: THOSE WHO SUPPORT ME IN MY FAITH

What Menu?

Read Luke 11:9–13

To [the One] who is able to do immeasurably more than all we ask or imagine... to him be glory.

Ephesians 3:20 (NIV)

'What are our chances of ordering something that is not on the menu?' As I finished speaking, the expression on the waiter's face said, 'Are you kidding? You want to order something that is not on the menu?' He looked at me as if it were clear I could not honestly expect that.

But I was serious. I asked him to check, and I was able to order something that was not on the menu. The cook had no problem in preparing it, and I paid a fair price.

When we pray, we can pray knowing that God does not answer only the prayers that are 'on the menu'. We see our situation and think about what we want from the Lord. We may pray with specific answers in mind, limiting the Lord to a 'menu'. We forget the words of Jesus, 'What is impossible for mortals is possible for God' (Luke 18:27, NRSV) and also 'With God all things are possible' (Matthew 19:26, NIV)!

Jesus taught that we can ask God for anything (John 14:13–14). However, while making our requests known to God is right, we can remember that God is able to answer our prayers in ways we never thought about. We restrict our prayer life when we ask God for answers so specific that we close our eyes to some other response.

Prayer: *Dear Lord, remind us that you see and give beyond anything we can even imagine. Thank you for answers to our prayers. Amen*

Thought for the day: God's ability to answer our prayers has no limits.

Jonathan Ibarra (Texas, US)

PRAYER FOCUS: RESTAURANT WAITERS

Play on Through

Read Psalm 34:1–14

Let us not become weary in doing good, for at the proper time we will reap a harvest if we do not give up.
Galatians 6:9 (NIV)

I live in a quiet cul-de-sac where the young neighbourhood boys, wearing roller skates, put up large nets and play hockey in the road. Just the other day, a cold rain poured down on them in the middle of the game. But there was no stopping them. Listening to their chatter, peppered with shouts, I couldn't help but delight in their enthusiasm and determination. Though soaked to the skin, they continued to skate, eager to score the next goal.

Recently 'cold rain' has come into my life in more ways than I feel I can handle. But God used those boys to remind me that I want to keep on skating too. I want to have the same faith to keep trying, eager to reach the next goal in my journey with Christ—no matter how uncomfortable my situation may be just now.

Prayer: *Dear heavenly Father, strengthen us and deliver us from our troubles. Help us not to give up but to lean on you, remembering that storms can lead to rainbows. We give you all the glory as we pray, 'Our Father which art in heaven, Hallowed be thy name. Thy kingdom come. Thy will be done in earth, as it is in heaven. Give us this day our daily bread. And forgive us our debts, as we forgive our debtors. And lead us not into temptation, but deliver us from evil: For thine is the kingdom, and the power, and the glory, for ever.'* Amen*

Thought for the day: God helps us to play through the rain.

Christine A. Setlock (New York, US)

 PRAYER FOCUS: YOUNG ATHLETES

* Matthew 6:9–13 (KJV)

Handmade

Read Psalm 139:13–18

When my bones were being formed, carefully put together in my mother's womb, when I was growing there in secret, you knew that I was there.
Psalm 139:15 (GNB)

My great-grandmother used to sit for hours knitting and crocheting. I most remember her making what she called 'doilies'. For those who don't know, a doily is a decorative mat, usually made of lace or linen. My grandmother placed them on the backs of chairs or on tables under a lamp or a bowl.

These doilies had very intricate patterns and took a great deal of time to make. They could not be mass-produced; each one was painstakingly and lovingly made. Bit by bit, my great-grandmother's creations took shape. She knew every thread, every stitch and every fibre of that doily.

The psalmist tells us that God has fashioned us with the same attention and care that my great-grandmother showed as she fashioned her doilies. God made each one of us individually and uniquely. With painstaking and loving care, God has knit us together. He knows each of us more intimately and thoroughly than my great-grandmother knew her doilies.

From the beginning, God has known us. He has knitted each of us together with love and patience for a special purpose. Each of us is handmade by God.

Prayer: *Help us remember, dear God, that you know us inside and out. Amen*

Thought for the day: Because God made us, he knows us and loves us.

Mike Morelan (Alabama, US)

A Secure Future

Read Matthew 6:25–34

Father of orphans and protector of widows is God in his holy habitation.

Psalm 68:5 (NRSV)

My father died in 1989. Suddenly my world became dark. I had never imagined that he would leave us so soon. At that time, my sister and I were still at college, and my mother had never worked outside our home. My father had been our guide—a firm family leader but patient, protective and full of tenderness. Suffering from our loss, we began to lose hope. We asked many questions. Can we survive? How can we meet our daily responsibilities? Can my sister and I finish our studies? Can Mum give us what we need?

Then the Bible passage above came to mind. I realised that we could feel secure only by giving our lives to God. As we did, God helped us. Our uncle financed our time at college until we graduated. My mother was able to sell her homemade biscuits, cakes and other food to our neighbours and relatives.

Twenty years have passed, and we all have learned to surrender our lives to God. Though my father is no longer with us as our guide and protector, God has become our father. We do not have to worry about our future; it's in God's hands.

Prayer: *We lift up our praise and gratitude to you, dear heavenly Father, because you are always with us. You help us when we lose hope. You chase away our fear and anxiety. Thank you. Amen*

Thought for the day: When we lose hope, we can find it again in God's caring presence.

Lautan Asima Basaria Siregar (Jakarta, Indonesia)

 PRAYER FOCUS: FAMILIES GRIEVING THE DEATH OF A PARENT

A New Life

Read Mark 1:9–13

We were... buried with [Christ] through baptism into death in order that, just as Christ was raised from the dead through the glory of the Father, we too may live a new life.

Romans 6:4 (NIV)

Those of us who have been baptised are excited about acknowledging God's grace but also concerned about the future. What changes will our profession of faith require of us? Exactly how are we to handle things differently now that we have submitted to God's will (or at least committed to learn how to do so)? How do we learn to rely on grace?

Jesus Christ must have felt some of the same concern as he looked to his future. As part of the Godhead, he was familiar with dealing with the world. But in human skin, Jesus probably felt some of the same anxiety—and maybe even some of the resistance—that you or I might feel about facing our futures. Yet despite any anxiety or resistance Jesus might have felt, he submitted to being baptised 'to fulfil all righteousness' (Matthew 3:15). As soon as he emerged from the water, Jesus, the human, got to feel the exhilaration of the Father's approval. Not long after, he also suffered temptation. Later he began to translate his commitment into action.

We see here that water is central to God's covenant with us, a soothing balm for our worries. Baptism serves as an earthly reminder of God's gentle, indestructible and powerful gift of grace and of God's promise to be with us as we fulfil the missions of our lives.

Prayer: *O God, we want to please you, but we also fear what is in store for us if we truly submit to your will. Help us to rely on you, your promises and your grace. Amen*

Thought for the day: What reminds me of God's grace day by day?

Terrell M. McDaniel (Tennessee, US)

God Means For Ever

Read Psalm 136:1–9, 23–26

Enter [the Lord's] gates with thanksgiving and his courts with praise; give thanks to him and praise his name. For the Lord is good and his love endures forever; his faithfulness continues through all generations.

Psalm 100:4–5 (NIV)

When I was a little girl, my father promised to love me for ever. But a few years later, he left our family. I grew up and got married. My husband promised to love me for ever; but in time, he too left our family. Unfortunately, experience has taught many of us that when people use the words 'for ever', they really mean 'for as long as it makes me happy' or 'until you fail to meet my expectations'. For many of us, having someone love us for ever has become a romantic notion that rarely happens in real life.

That's why I'm glad that someone truly means, 'I will love you for ever.' For God, 'for ever' doesn't mean 'for as long as you please me' or 'just until you mess things up'. The words 'his love endures for ever' appear more than 40 times in the Bible. And this is more than just a promise. It is a truth about God's nature. God will always be steadfast in loving us, because love is who God is. And that means God really will love us for ever.

Prayer: *Thank you, God, for loving us even when we feel unlovable. Help us to remember that you always love us. Amen*

Thought for the day: No matter how we may fail God, he will never fail us.

Diane Stark (Indiana, US)

What's in My Heart?

Read Matthew 15:10–20

What comes out of the mouth proceeds from the heart, and this is what defiles.

Matthew 15:18 (NRSV)

'Watch out!' I screamed and then jumped back as a little boy bumped into me while trying to kick a bouncing football. Annoyance bubbled up inside me as I looked at the spreading coffee stain on my new cream jacket. Fortunately, I didn't have time to say anything to the child as he raced off after the ball, oblivious to the minor accident he had caused.

'Why doesn't someone keep those kids under control?' I muttered, sounding like my grandmother many years ago. Later I wondered why I had reacted so strongly. After all, he was just a little child playing football. He didn't intend any harm.

I hadn't given any thought to my reaction; it just spilled out, much like that coffee. Jesus once warned his disciples that what came out of their mouths actually came from their hearts.

The Bible reminds us repeatedly to be joyful. If my heart is full of joy, when I'm knocked off balance, joy will spill out. If my heart is full of love, when something or someone bumps into me, I will react in love. I resolved to be more careful about what I put into my heart because I want what spills out to be joy.

Prayer: *Loving Father, forgive us for the times our hearts have overflowed in harmful ways. Help us to bring healing and blessing to those around us, even when we're knocked off balance. Amen*

Thought for the day: When our hearts are filled with love, life's little collisions will not harm us and those near us.

Shirley M. Corder (Eastern Cape, South Africa)

House of God

Read Psalm 84

Let us consider how to provoke one another to love and good deeds, not neglecting to meet together, as is the habit of some, but encouraging one another, and all the more as you see the Day approaching.
Hebrews 10:24–25 (NRSV)

Because I grew up in a nation under Communist rule, going to church wasn't my custom. But in my early 20s I began to seek God. God led me to a place where people confessed and worshipped Christ as their Saviour and Lord. I liked the fellowship, but I was concerned what other people would think of me. Further, my family strongly objected to my going to church. Conflict grew inside me.

Sometimes I went to church, only to feel ashamed because attending church was considered insane in an ungodly country. It took seven years before I could attend church freely. What joy and peace it brought me!

For many reasons, God wants believers to meet together. The most important reason is that God has never intended for us to live separated from one another. People aren't perfect, but God is. In church, we are perfected as we study the Bible, take part in corporate praise and worship, pray with other believers and spend time with one another. That's how we live our daily lives to the fullest, in God's will and for his glory.

Prayer: *Dear Jesus, we thank you for your Church. Amen*

Thought for the day: 'I was glad when they said to me, "Let us go to the house of the Lord!"' (see Psalm 122:1).

Yulia Bagwell (Pennsylvania, US)

Leave the Rest to God

Read Genesis 37:1–8

Not that I have already... been made perfect, but I press on to take hold of that for which Christ Jesus took hold of me.

Philippians 3:12 (NIV)

Let's face it: none of our families are perfect. I've seen some great ones, but even at their very best none of them matches up to the 'perfect' kind of family we see on TV.

Fortunately, however, few of our families reach the level of dysfunction we find in Jacob's clan. As if having twelve sons born to two wives and two concubines wasn't complicated enough, added to the family mix was Jacob's favouritism toward his best-loved wife, Rachel, and her two sons, Joseph and Benjamin. Mix in a dose of Joseph's arrogance and it's no wonder the other brothers wanted to kill him. That was a family at perhaps its worst.

But even when we are at our best, we will not be able to heal every broken relationship, tie up every loose end and reach some sort of perfection in the relationships in our families, our friendships, in our community and even in the Body of Christ.

I've heard people say that they want to be like Jesus, expressing perfect, limitless love in difficult relationships. That is, after all, where discipleship leads us. But while God's love is perfect, limitless and unending, ours is not. Our loving will always be limited by our human imperfections. The best we can do is to love the best we can and leave the rest to God's grace.

Prayer: *Thank you, God, that your love for us is perfect. Amen*

Thought for the day: God calls us to seek perfection, not to attain it.

James A. Harnish (Florida, US)

PRAYER FOCUS: MY FAMILY

Perfectly Attuned

Read John 3:22–30

Jesus said, 'Abide in me as I abide in you. Just as the branch cannot bear fruit by itself unless it abides in the vine, neither can you unless you abide in me.'

John 15:4 (NRSV)

While I was listening to a recording of traditional flute music of the Andes Mountains, I marvelled at how perfectly the accompanying piano blended with the flute. The piano contributed while remaining in the background so that the flute was predominant. There was no doubt which musician was the soloist. The pianist did not compete with the flautist.

My thoughts turned to how John the Baptist countered the concerns of his friends who thought that Jesus was competing with him in gaining new disciples. John said unequivocally, 'He [Jesus] must increase, but I must decrease.' John played a significant role in calling people to repentance and drawing their attention to Jesus, preparing the way for them to accept our Lord's teaching. But John refused to seek acclaim for himself or to compete with Jesus for attention.

We too are to keep in harmony with Christ, not competing with him but depending on him to lead us so that other people may see and hear our Lord and Saviour.

Prayer: *Thank you, Jesus, for moments that lead us to deeper understanding of what you have taught us. Help us always to abide in you. Amen*

Thought for the day: We are not the stars in making the music of faith; Christ is.

Hazel V. Thompson (Somerset, England)

God Cares

Read Psalm 23

[God] has said, 'I will never leave you or forsake you.'

Hebrews 13:5 (NRSV)

Have you ever known a person who seems never to be serious? Who never seems to pay any attention to anything? I know somebody who fits this description entirely: my friend Jeff. We're at college together. Jeff has failed Spanish three times and couldn't care less about it. You might think Jeff would treat people the same way. But I've known Jeff since primary school, and I know that's not true. Every time someone is sad or needs help, Jeff does what he can to make them feel better. I, for one, know I can count on Jeff.

In some ways I think God is like my friend Jeff. There are times I wonder if God is paying attention to me. I can never be absolutely sure. But I'm 99 per cent certain God is because whenever I pray, I feel as though I'm not alone. Even though it may seem like God isn't paying attention, he leads us and listens to us when we need it most.

Prayer: *Thank you, God, for friends who care for us. Thank you that even though we sometimes wonder if you're there, your love constantly surrounds us. Amen*

Thought for the day: Regardless of how we feel, God is close to us and cares.

Tommy Warrick (Virginia, US)

Answering the Call

Read Mark 2:1–12

'I was hungry and you fed me, thirsty and you gave me a drink; I was a stranger and you received me in your homes, naked and you clothed me. I was sick and you took care of me, in prison and you visited me.'

Matthew 25:35–36 (GNB)

I work in a physical therapy unit. I see people whose lives have been irrevocably changed by stroke, brain injury or debilitating disease such as cancer. I feel that on some days I witness miracles as I see a patient's progress; on other days, I am saddened to think that a patient may be as well physically as he or she is going to get. Patients and their families face physical challenges and lifestyle changes. Everything is different for them; nothing will ever be the same. I think about the people placed in my care, and I feel privileged to be part of their healing.

When I struggle, I remember that God placed me in this facility to work with these people. I also remember that as Christians, we are called to bring strength to the weak, rest to the weary and hope to those who despair. Remembering that we belong to Christ, we answer the call to serve those near us, wherever we are.

Prayer: *Dear God, we ask that as we do daily tasks we may honour and glorify you. We hold the sick, the weak, the weary and the despairing before you in prayer. Amen*

Thought for the day: Answering God's call to serve leads to life's greatest reward.

Link2Life: *Think about volunteering as a hospital visitor.*

Sherry Brooks Martin (South Carolina, US)

Darkness or Light?

Read John 3:16–21

I do not do the good I want, but the evil I do not want is what I do.
Romans 7:19 (NRSV)

I like to ride my bicycle along a familiar route that follows a circuit of seven or eight miles. When I reach one point, I have to decide whether to turn right and continue into the countryside or turn left and return home. One day as I reached the point of decision, I looked toward home and saw black clouds with occasional lightning and thunder. When I looked to the right, away from home, the sky was blue with only occasional light clouds. I continued on my longer route and returned home later without feeling a single drop of rain. That decision was easy.

While Jesus was on earth, he spoke of a similar decision between light and darkness. Why is that decision not as easy in our daily lives as it was for me that day on my bicycle? Jesus said that it is because our actions are evil and we fear exposure. We prefer to stay in the dark and stumble—again and again. However, Jesus is the light. If we choose to stay in darkness and avoid the light, we separate ourselves from Jesus. When we turn toward the light, we can enjoy the way of living that Christ offers us. We have a choice: we can stumble in the dark or walk in the light.

Prayer: *Dear heavenly Father, grant us the wisdom, strength and will to walk in your light instead of the world's darkness. Amen*

Thought for the day: Every day brings opportunities to choose God's way.

Ted Beemer (Dominican Republic)

Divine Comfort

Read 2 Corinthians 1:3–7

Blessed be the God and Father of our Lord Jesus Christ, the Father of mercies and the God of all consolation, who consoles us in all our affliction, so that we may be able to console those who are in any affliction.

2 Corinthians 1:3–4 (NRSV)

One evening not long ago, I was surprised to receive a text message from a teenager. The news was not good. A friend had died in a car accident. The teenager's despair and heartache were nearly palpable. I was asked to pray, and I agreed.

In the days that followed, I held this teenager and an entire community in my prayers. I received another text message 24 hours following the accident, asking for words from scripture that could offer comfort. I suggested 2 Corinthians 1:3–7. There Paul offers the church a word of comfort. He does not deny their struggles; rather, he acknowledges their suffering and pain. He reminds them that God responds to us in our persecution and affliction. Even as Paul embraces their pain, he points beyond suffering to ultimate hope.

As I considered the suffering of my young friends, I encouraged them to lean on God, who through Christ brings comfort and the strength to endure.

Prayer: *Dear Jesus, help us to receive your comfort in the midst of our pain, for you have borne our burdens, extended us grace and offered us healing through your cross. In you we have hope. Amen*

Thought for the day: Lean on God, who offers us comfort in all our pain.

Link2Life: *Form a prayer circle to pray for hurting people in your community.*

Benjamin Simpson (Kansas, US)

Give Thanks

Read Luke 17:11–19

May the peoples praise you, O God; may all the peoples praise you.
Psalm 67:3 (NIV)

I was reared in the 1940s and 50s in a small Mississippi Delta town, in a wonderful school system. My classmates and I were taught at an early age to be thankful for even the smallest gifts and to respond with handwritten notes of appreciation. Our parents and English teachers taught us well. For years, I have continued to write thank-you notes, even though, as I age, tremors in my hands make writing difficult. I tried teaching my children by example. Consequently, I become disheartened when I give a gift of love and do not receive acknowledgment, either in a handwritten note or a telephone call.

But how often do I take the time to give thanks to our heavenly Father, who has given us so much? Every day God blesses us with bountiful goodness. Do we remember to give thanks to him for everything we have? Or do we pray only when we need something? I imagine that our heavenly Father delights in our giving thanks and praise for all we have, perhaps especially for the small gifts.

Prayer: *Dear heavenly Father, you richly bless us every day with life and with the beauty of creation. Help us to remember to praise and thank you for the gifts you have given to us. We pray as Jesus taught us, saying, 'Our Father which art in heaven, Hallowed be thy name. Thy kingdom come. Thy will be done, as in heaven, so in earth. Give us day by day our daily bread. And forgive us our sins; for we also forgive every one that is indebted to us. And lead us not into temptation; but deliver us from evil.'* Amen*

Thought for the day: Gratitude is a joyful way of life.

June E. Nixon (Mississippi, US)

PRAYER FOCUS: FOR MORE GRATEFUL HEARTS

* Luke 11:2–4 (KJV)

God's Soil

Read Matthew 13:1–9, 18–23

I am confident of this, that the one who began a good work among you will bring it to completion by the day of Jesus Christ.
Philippians 1:6 (NRSV)

I love planting things, especially flowers. Last summer I dug up the flowerbed in the communal garden of the multi-storey flats where I live. This took a lot of effort, but it was worth it. A month later a multi-coloured variety of beautiful flowers started to bloom, delighting the inhabitants of the flats and passersby. For the next month, the flowerbed brought beauty to our courtyard. Every day children with watering cans came out to water the flowers.

But one morning, we discovered that during the night someone had taken away our flowers. The empty flowerbed filled me with despair. All my labour had been in vain. I was really angry and decided that it was pointless for me to plant flowers.

Then I began to think about how God works in our life. We are the soil in which God sows and cultivates the seeds of faith. We start to blossom and bear fruit, bringing joy to God and blessings to other people. When the devil begins to prowl around us and removes from our hearts the seeds of faith, God continues to sow and cultivate. Knowing this, I planted flowers again. I will keep on planting and cultivating them over and over again—taking my example from our loving and caring Lord.

Prayer: *Dear Lord, thank you for the seeds of faith that you continue to sow and cultivate in us. Amen*

Thought for the day: Because God never gives up on me, neither will I.

Natalia Prokhorova (Samara, Russia)

Use it for Good

Read Jeremiah 29:11–13

'I know the plans I have for you,' declares the Lord, 'plans to prosper you and not to harm you, plans to give you hope and a future.'
Jeremiah 29:11 (NIV)

I awake at five in the morning. My first clear thought sends me into despair. A phone call last night had confirmed my worst fears: my daughter has diabetes. My happy, loving eleven-year-old has a serious lifelong disease; and I can do nothing about it.

I search for information on the internet, but it only adds to my hopelessness. I turn to my Bible, where I read the words I need to embrace: ' "I know the plans I have for you," declares the Lord.' These words will help us through the uncertainty that lies ahead; I could feel their strength as I faced that first morning.

Ten years have passed, years filled with changing recipes, weighing food and giving injections while she played football, ran cross-country, figure-skated, and steadily took over responsibility for managing her disease. She is now a healthy, happy, active graduate student. God had plans for her future. He not only helped her to live well with the disease, but also gave her the grace and strength to make adjustments so that it never hindered the life he had planned for her. Thank God for holy words that lift us up when we are at our lowest!

Prayer: *Dear Lord, thank you for being with us when we have nowhere else to turn. Thank you for your holy word that lifts us out of despair and fills our hearts with peace. Amen*

Thought for the day: God's plan is better than anything we can imagine.

Sheryl L. Brown (Michigan, US)

PRAYER FOCUS: CHILDREN WITH DIABETES

Postcard from an Apostle

Read 1 John 1:1–4

We declare to you what we have seen and heard so that you… may have fellowship with us… so that our joy may be complete.

1 John 1:3–4 (NRSV)

When on trips, I send postcards to my friends. I want them to know I'm having a great time but also that it would be even more fun if they could be with me. And I sense the same message when I receive a postcard from someone dear.

That's the message the apostle John was sending in today's reading—not only to his beloved brothers and sisters two thousand years ago but to us as well. Having seen 'the word of life' with his own eyes, John lived with others who also knew and loved Jesus. The only thing that would make things better for him, he wrote, would be to share their fellowship. It's as if John is wishing we were there with them.

And we can be. No matter what distance separates us, whether miles or time, as God's family we are in fellowship with all believers—which makes our joy complete. And we can reach out with 'postcards' of our own by living the message of faith. When we share the gospel, we are telling someone else how much we want them to be with us—in fellowship with other believers and with Jesus Christ.

Prayer: *Complete our joy, heavenly Father. Let the good news of salvation be seen in our life together. Amen*

Thought for the day: Across all borders and barriers, God makes us one.

Frank Ramirez (Pennsylvania, US)

The T-shirt

Read Romans 7:14–25

May God be gracious to us and bless us and make his face to shine upon us, that your way may be known upon earth, your saving power among all nations.

Psalm 67:1–2 (NRSV)

One of the most riveting events of all time captured the attention of the entire world in 2010. Thirty-three miners were trapped in a copper mine in Chile. News reports gave minute-by-minute coverage of the monumental rescue effort.

I recall seeing the lettering on the T-shirts the rescued miners wore after they emerged. 'Jesus' was written on each sleeve, and 'Thank you, Lord' was printed on the front and back, along with a biblical reference. This was a way to thank God for the miracle of their survival in the depths of the mine and for being rescued.

Many months have elapsed now since the rescue. The media has mentioned little or nothing about the miners; they have ceased to be a news item. But I continue to think about the T-shirts, and I wonder if that immediate awareness of Christ continues in their hearts and in their lives.

As limited and real as this rescue experience was, we too are blessed because we are rescued by Christ. Most believers do not wear special T-shirts emblazoned with a message for all to see. But in our day-to-day living, do we keep Christ in our hearts? Are we continually, truly and profoundly grateful for our rescue 'from sin to salvation'?

Prayer: *Dear heavenly Father, may we remain ever grateful to you. In Jesus' name we pray. Amen*

Thought for the day: How do we show gratitude for our salvation?

Mila Roxana Guerrero Jaramillo (Biobío, Chile)

First Things

Read Micah 6:6–8

'But seek first his kingdom and his righteousness, and all these things will be given to you as well.'

Matthew 6:33 (NIV)

When I was a young man, I wanted to learn to cook. 'Cooking shouldn't be difficult,' I thought. 'After all, it looks simple when I watch others who know what they are doing.' One day, I tried to cook on my own. What followed was a series of mistakes and fiascos that might have been funny to anyone watching but filled me with frustration. I explained my problem to a friend. A day later, I received the gift of a beginners' cookery book. On the front page, my friend had written a note in bold letters: 'There are two rules. First, be sure you have all the ingredients. Second, read and follow the recipe instructions carefully.'

Cooking on my own, I had substituted ingredients, taken short cuts and got the cooking times wrong. After carefully reading the book, I successfully learned to cook simple dishes. The two rules sounded too easy, but following them worked.

Jesus told his followers to seek God first. Then everything else in their lives would come together properly. Many Christians try substitutions and shortcuts, or they get the timing wrong—all of which brings frustration. My friend's two rules might apply to Christian life. Begin with the essentials. Put God first. Then read and follow God's book carefully.

Prayer: *Dear God, lead us to turn to you daily for guidance and instruction. Help us to live in ways that bring justice and dignity to others. Amen*

Thought for the day: Put God first; then act in God's name.

Gale A. Richards (Iowa, US)

Love your Enemies

Read Luke 6:27–36

Jesus said, 'I say to you that listen, Love your enemies.'

Luke 6:27 (NRSV)

'Love your enemies.' What a difficult teaching! How do we love an enemy? Hearing these words and trying to practise them brings God into the hurt and pain and broken places of our lives. And we see faces. Enemies are those who have harmed us or threatened us. But how do we love such people?

Although no one has ever seriously harmed me or my family, I have experienced many threatening situations. And I know many people who have been greatly harmed in body or spirit by the actions of others. Our world needs these words of Jesus if we are to find lasting peace and understanding—a way of life and a way of love that can heal the wounds and bridge the gaps between us. God can help us choose to love rather than hate. Consequently, Jesus' words challenge us on levels that are real and uncomfortable. Sometimes it may seem easier to keep animosities alive than to love.

Whenever I read Jesus' words about loving our enemies, I ask myself: whom do I need to forgive? What old injuries or careless words need to be forgotten? Who is the enemy I need to love, and how can I show it? It's not easy, but today is a good day to begin a new life with an old enemy.

Prayer: *Dear God of all goodness, make us instruments of your peace, and show us how to love today. Amen*

Thought for the day: Today is a good day to begin forgiving.

Link2Life: *Learn more about, and pray for, world conflicts.*

Todd Outcalt (Indiana, US)

At the Feet of Jesus

Read Luke 10:38–42

'Martha, Martha,' the Lord answered, 'you are worried and upset about many things, but only one thing is needed.'

Luke 10:41-42 (NIV)

The phone rang. A church member had died, and I was asked to organise lunch for the family after the funeral. I had never done anything like this before. I felt overwhelmed and anxious. After a restless night, I arrived bleary-eyed in the church hall kitchen. People started arriving in groups, talking and laughing, to assist with the meal. They didn't seem overly concerned about the task at hand. We were able to get everything ready by the time the family members arrived. They were grateful, and I saw that all my worry had been unnecessary.

In the story of Mary and Martha, Martha spends her time in the kitchen preparing the meal. I was like Martha, overwhelmed by preparations and worried about getting the work done. Mary chose the better way by sitting at the feet of Jesus, listening to his words.

At times we worry about performing our tasks more than focusing on our Lord. The better thing is to stop and listen to Jesus. Since we cannot literally sit at Jesus' feet, we can ask the help of the Holy Spirit. The Spirit helps us to pray, to understand scripture, to relate to others, and to be more Christ-like in our love. In becoming more like Mary, I can be a better Martha.

Prayer: *God, when we give in to anxiety, show us a better way. Amen*

Thought for the day: How did I spend time listening to Jesus today?

Michelle A. Wilson (North Carolina, US)

Interested in You

Read James 2:1–8

I praise you, for I am fearfully and wonderfully made.

Psalm 139:14 (NRSV)

Compared to many in my new school, I was from 'the wrong side of town'. I had to catch two buses to attend school, while many of my classmates arrived in luxury cars. Being on time or staying for extra activities was difficult for me if one of the buses was late. Making friends was a struggle. I felt that I was judged to be not good enough when some girls discovered where I lived, what my father did for a living or that my mother had no career outside the home. I began to pray that God would give me a friend. In time, God did give me a new friend and later a whole group of friends.

Neither my parents nor my brother were able to finish their schooling, but they went without things to give me an opportunity to complete my education. Eventually, I qualified as a teacher and later as a minister. The key to my achievements was discovering that God not only listens to our prayers but accepts all of us—even me.

I am glad that God does not value us according to where we live, how educated we may or may not be or our material wealth. God simply loves us and longs to be in a loving relationship with us.

Prayer: *Dear Lord, thank you for your interest in each of us, regardless of who we are or where we come from. Amen*

Thought for the day: God loves you just as you are.

Jeanette Krige (Gauteng, South Africa)

PRAYER FOCUS: TEENAGERS STRUGGLING TO MAKE FRIENDS

Being There

Read 1 Corinthians 13:4–7

'My grace is sufficient for you, for my power is made perfect in weakness.'
2 Corinthians 12:9 (NIV)

Following a major operation for neck cancer my husband, Mike, became severely depressed. Towards the end of his three-week stay in hospital he confessed to feeling suicidal. However, the medical team felt his recovery would be best aided at home and he was duly discharged. Despite their confidence I had very mixed feelings as we drove home.

While I prepared a meal that evening, Mike sat dejectedly at the table. Then, above the cooking clatter, I heard a strange rattling sound. I turned and was shocked to see Mike shaking so badly he was making the table jump.

Who was this pale, frightened stranger? Where was the kind, gentle man I had known and loved for 28 years? I felt totally inadequate and ill-prepared for the role that had been thrust upon me. 'Help!' was my silent prayer.

'Just love him,' came the calm, reassuring answer.

During the months that followed there were many testing times. Heeding God's straightforward advice I cared for Mike as best I could, trying to allay his irrational fears, to tolerate his erratic behaviour and be encouraging and supportive. I often struggled to understand and was frustrated by his unresponsiveness, all the while feeling desperately sorry for his painful predicament.

St Paul's wonderful description of love, particularly the first and last sentences of today's reading, was and remains inspirational.

Prayer: *Thank you, Lord, for your amazing promise to share our burdens and lighten our load.*

Thought for the day: As God is there for us, so may we be for others.

Linda Hunter (Co. Durham, England)

The Good Way

Read 1 Samuel 12:19–25

The prophet Samuel said to the people of Israel, 'I will teach you the way that is good and right.'

1 Samuel 12:23 (NIV)

Duncan sat across from me with his head bowed. He was in trouble. As a primary school administrator, I often talk to pupils who are in trouble. On this afternoon, Duncan's teacher had asked me to speak with Duncan about his behaviour in the cafeteria. I asked Duncan what had happened, and he admitted that he had thrown food at several students simply because he thought it would be fun. When I asked him whether he had made a good choice, he shook his head from side to side and began to cry.

We continued talking about good and right choices, and Duncan decided that he would make a good choice by writing an apology letter to the students he had hit. At the end of our conversation, Duncan also assured me that in the future he would make better decisions about his behaviour.

As Christians, we are called to make choices every day. Since we belong to Christ, we need not despair about making these decisions because the Bible assures us that God will give us wisdom about what is good and right (see James 1:5).

Prayer: *Dear Lord, teach us your good way and give us courage to follow it. Amen*

Thought for the day: God faithfully gives us guidance when we ask for it.

James C. Hendrix (Indiana, US)

Shattered

Read 1 Corinthians 15:42–48

O Lord, my God, I called to you for help and you healed me.

Psalm 30:2 (NIV)

A few years ago, I fell in a car park and shattered my left wrist. Not long after that, I lost my job. Then a sister-in-law, two brothers, two close friends and my father died. I felt that my life and my spirit were as shattered as my wrist.

While going through physical therapy for my wrist and hand, I spent time with God in meditation and Bible reading; I also got more involved in the church. As my body healed, so did my spirit.

Though the broken bone healed, I cannot bend the fingers on my left hand. When my grandson, Logan, commented on this, I told him my fingers remind me that when we fall physically or spiritually, God is there to pick us up and put us back together. Logan kissed my hand and said, 'When you get to heaven, God will give you a brand new hand!'

God has promised us eternal life without pain or sorrow, where all things will be made new. Whether our hurts are physical, emotional or spiritual, God can and does make us whole again.

Prayer: *Dear God, mould and shape us into the people you mean us to be. Amen*

Thought for the day: God puts us back together when we are falling apart.

Elaine S. Clark (Georgia, US)

Home and Helper

Read John 14:1–17

'Do not let your hearts be troubled.'

John 14:1 (NIV)

Last week I travelled to my home town. The trip was not pleasant. We endured bumpy roads, irritating neighbours, a boring film and crowded seating. But in spite of all these difficulties, I was able to enjoy my travel for two reasons. First, I knew that the next morning I would be at home. Second, my wife was by my side. She always wants to help me; she assists me in all that I do. I talk about how I feel, and she understands and encourages me. She is a good helper. The confidence that I would reach my home and the comfort of having a helper at my side made my journey joyful and kept me on course.

Jesus assured his disciples of similar help and comfort, promising a home and a helper. He knew that dark days were awaiting him and his friends, but still he said, 'Do not let your hearts be troubled.' Jesus encouraged them with the promises that he was going to prepare a place for them in heaven and that the Father would send the Holy Spirit to be their advocate and Comforter.

We have those same assurances today. The balm for troubled hearts is remembering that we have a place in heaven and accepting the comfort and guidance of the Holy Spirit, our helper and companion as we journey home.

Prayer: *Dear Father, thank you for the promise of a home in heaven at the end of our journey. And thank you for your constant presence with us through the Holy Spirit. Amen*

Thought for the day: The Holy Spirit is a constant companion on our journey.

Daniel Kingsly (Tamil Nadu, India)

A Refreshing Spray

Read Isaiah 44:3–8

[Those who do not listen to the wicked] are like trees planted by streams of water, which yield their fruit in its season.
Psalm 1:3 (NRSV)

Several years ago, I travelled to Zimbabwe on a work assignment. The country was experiencing a terrible drought that year. All along the road we could see the devastating results—the dusty, dried-out fields containing no vegetation, the carcasses of thousands of livestock strewn across the countryside. However, when we reached legendary Victoria Falls, I saw an incredible sight. The forest in the immediate vicinity was as green and lush as anything I had ever seen. I soon learned the reason: the natural spray from the river, as it plunges over the high cliffs of the falls, literally creates a constant 'rain' or mist over the area that results in spectacular foliage.

The presence of that lush rainforest in the midst of such a devastating drought revealed a profound truth: we too can live in the midst of drought, not a drought of water but a drought of compassion, understanding and love. This inner drought leaves us as thirsty and hopeless as the bony farm animals on the side of the road in Zimbabwe. The refreshment we need comes from God, who ministers to our drought-weary hearts through a song, the kind words of a friend, an unexpected telephone call or a note sent through the post. Bathed in God's love, we become part of the stream ourselves, flowing to and nurturing others. Those ever-flowing streams bathe us in the refreshing spray of God's love and care.

Prayer: *Dear Lord, help us to receive your life-giving water today. In Jesus' name we pray. Amen*

Thought for the day: Who needs me to offer God's life-giving water today?

Hilly Hicks (Tennessee, US)

Between God and Me

Read Matthew 25:31–46

The king will answer them, 'Truly I tell you, just as you did it to one of the least of these who are members of my family, you did it to me.'

Matthew 25:40 (NRSV)

While driving home from Philadelphia, my wife and I stopped at a red light before crossing the bridge into southern New Jersey. At the light was a poor man wearing rosaries and carrying a bucket of soapy water and a sponge. He started to wash the car's front window. I yelled at him to stop and told him that I would not pay him for his labour. The poor man explained that he had to work to eat; if I did not want to pay him, that was between God and me.

My wife pulled out a dollar and gave it to him when he finished his job and the light turned green. My wife was shocked by my behaviour and said that turning down someone in need was not like me. She then recited Matthew 25:40. I was speechless; I knew she was right and that I had sinned.

As we pulled into our driveway at home, I realised that I am blessed and that others need help from those more fortunate. Since this incident, I have been more generous toward those in need. I hope and pray that I am never so tight-fisted again.

Prayer: *O God of forgiveness and understanding, thank you for forgiving our sins. Help us to be more generous and to give to those less fortunate than we are. Let us remember to treat our brothers and sisters as we would treat you. Amen*

Thought for the day: Christ comes to us in every needy person.

Steven Philipp (New Jersey, US)

PRAYER FOCUS: THE HOMELESS

Spiritual Friends

Read Galatians 6:1–5

If anyone is detected in a transgression, you who have received the Spirit should restore such a one in a spirit of gentleness.

Galatians 6:1 (NRSV)

I had taken a rock-wall-climbing challenge as a dare, despite my fear of heights. As my fingers found themselves placed in the climbing holes, my mind raced. What would happen if I fell? Would someone be there to catch me? I cautiously peered down the 36-foot wall and spotted the belayer—the person who controls the tension in the rope. Belayers give climbers slack in the rope when it's needed and pull in excess to prevent a fall. Then I was not so fearful.

In a spiritual sense, God gives us belayers in life. They may be friends, mentors or spiritual directors. God gives us relationships that encourage us upward in our spiritual growth and keep us from stumbling. These people comfort and care for us but also hold us accountable for how we live our faith.

We may feel hurt or offended when someone we love points out a shortcoming. However, spiritual friends love us in spite of our faults and challenge us to change, to grow closer to the way of Christ.

Prayer: *Dear God, thank you for those who hold us accountable. Open our hearts and minds to accept your loving correction and make us willing to change. Amen*

Thought for the day: Loving Christians hold each other accountable.

Cary Tabares (Florida, US)

One in Christ Jesus

Read Galatians 3:24–29

There is no longer Jew or Greek, there is no longer slave or free, there is no longer male and female; for all of you are one in Christ Jesus.
Galatians 3:28 (NRSV)

My family and I went to church one Sunday for worship and Communion. Among the visitors was a man who appeared to be Asian. We did not understand his language, and he did not understand ours. Verbal communication seemed impossible.

When the pastor presented visitors to the congregation, the man stood and greeted us with a friendly wave of his hand, smiling effusively. When the call to the Lord's Table was given, I concluded that while unable to understand all the words of the pastor, the visitor knew the universal language of the Communion liturgy.

As I meditated during Communion, I remembered the Bible's words, 'Let mutual love continue. Do not neglect to show hospitality to strangers' (Hebrews 13:1–2). I walked up to stand beside the man and gave him a warm embrace as we wept and took Communion together. With a gesture indicating his gratitude, he smiled at me. Our oneness in Christ overcame our differences and filled us with joy.

Prayer: *Loving God, help us practise hospitality and to show by our actions that we all are one in Christ Jesus. Amen*

Thought for the day: Those who follow Christ always have a place at God's table.

María M. Urdaz (Puerto Rico)

God's Promise

Read Isaiah 43:1–4

Jesus said, 'Surely, I am with you always.'

Matthew 28:20 (NIV)

Looking out of the dining-room window in the early morning while having my coffee is one of my favourite moments of the day. I see the glow of the sun as it shines through the southern pines, and I see the trees' reflection on a nearby lake.

In contrast to this peaceful scene, many nations are struggling with serious economic problems. Now in middle age, I sometimes worry that budget cuts will force my department to be downsized or my job to be terminated. With a family to care for, I would find such a change to be a terrible burden. But this morning as I look out the window at God's beautiful creation, I see on our dining table a small figure of a smiling Jesus with outstretched arms. The figure, which my daughter Meagan made some time ago, seemed to be saying, 'Don't be afraid. I am here, and I always will be.' A peace came over me that is hard to describe.

God never promises that our lives will be free of worry, hardship or pain. But God does promise always to be with us, through good times and bad.

Prayer: *Dear heavenly Father, thank you for always being with us. Help us to trust you more. We pray this in Jesus' holy name. Amen*

Thought for the day: 'Faith is being sure of what we hope for and certain of what we do not see' (Hebrews 11:1).

Charles Kimbrough (Georgia, US)

 PRAYER FOCUS: THOSE FEARING JOB LOSS

Abundant Provision

Read 1 Timothy 6:17–21

Taste and see that the Lord is good.

Psalm 34:8 (NRSV)

My two sons were out playing tennis when I had to leave the house. I left them a note in large handwriting, 'Ham sandwiches for lunch'. Near the sign was a covered dish of meat, a jar of mustard and a loaf of bread. When I got home several hours later, I found the lunch untouched. On top of the sign sat an opened can of tuna fish and a box of crackers. Later I asked Sam about lunch. He admitted it was terrible, eating tuna from the can with crackers, 'But we couldn't find anything else.' Abundant provisions had been at hand. The table was laid out. The instructions were plain. The only thing missing was the simple act of recognising the gift and taking it.

In a similar vein, how many times do we miss the wonderful gifts God longs to give us? Too often we don't listen closely enough to understand God's directions for us. Too often we are not ready and willing to hear what God says. Thus we miss out on the real joys of a Spirit-filled life. But through the disciplines of scripture reading, prayer and regular worship, we can learn to see, appreciate and use what God has given us.

Prayer: *Dear Lord, help us to notice and receive the blessings you want to give us. Keep us spiritually alert to your will and your way. Amen*

Thought for the day: God's giving extends far beyond all we can imagine.

Joy C. Eastridge (Tennessee, US)

A Powerful God

Read Nahum 1:6–9 and Romans 3:21–26

A jealous and avenging God is the Lord, the Lord is avenging and wrathful; the Lord takes vengeance on his adversaries and rages against his enemies.

Nahum 1:2 (NRSV)

I find it difficult to read words like the ones spoken by the prophet Nahum. Words like 'anger', 'wrath', 'indignation' and 'vengeance' seem far removed from the words I like to associate with God. However, reading such passages also helps me to remember how much God loves me.

Really, I am no better than the Ninevites addressed in today's reading from Nahum. Like them, I plot against God in my heart and by my actions. I reason, 'This isn't specifically forbidden in the Bible, so it must be OK.' At the same time, I try to ignore the Holy Spirit who is telling me, 'No!'

However, despite my wilful disobedience and sin, God chose to save me. Before time began, God looked across the expanse of time and space: he saw the sins of Nineveh; he saw my sins; he saw all the sins of the world. However, God has said over and over, 'I will redeem my people.' Jesus died because we sin, to save us from the wrath of a God who hates sin.

God still hates our sin and sees it as the enemy. But instead of directing fury and wrath at us, God counts us righteous because of Jesus.

Prayer: *Thank you, O God, that you are slow to anger and quick to forgive when we turn to you. Help us always to remember what Jesus did for us. Amen*

Thought for the day: Our righteous God readily forgives our unrighteousness.

Leona Matson (British Columbia, Canada)

Choose Joy

Read Jonah 3:1—4:5

Be kind to one another, tenderhearted, forgiving one another, as God in Christ has forgiven you.

Ephesians 4:32 (NRSV)

Most of us have experienced trials when we wanted to blame God for something. Jonah was no exception. He was angry because God had shown mercy on a city known for its wickedness. Jonah's attitude was anything but forgiving. Expecting to see God rain fire and brimstone on the great city of Nineveh, he instead saw 'God graciously allow the city to stand'.

Forgiving a person or a group of people is hard if they have greatly wronged us; we often harbour anger and bitterness. We may become suspicious and paranoid, letting that wrong affect every area of our lives. Resentment can damage our bodies like a poison and destroy our relationships. Ironically, our resentment does not harm those who have injured us. We hurt only ourselves.

On the other hand, forgiving others neutralises the poisons of anger and bitterness. Instead of misery, we can choose joy. We go on without the heavy burden of anger. Our reward for developing a spirit of love is happiness. We begin to appreciate the gifts of God. We learn to value the days God gives us, and we can live every area of life to the fullest. When we possess a grateful and forgiving heart, outside circumstances cannot diminish the joy in each day.

Prayer: *Wonderful Father, thank you for helping us to see beyond the turmoil that sometimes rages around and within us. Amen*

Thought for the day: Forgiving is the antidote to the poison of bitterness.

James E. Bell (Missouri, US)

PRAYER FOCUS: SOMEONE I NEED TO FORGIVE

Showers of Blessing

Read Psalm 103:1–13

[The Lord] does not treat us as our sins deserve or repay us according to our iniquities.

Psalm 103:10 (NIV)

It rained in my neighbour's garden today. That's not unusual, except that it didn't rain in mine. The scattered showers that interrupted our Texas drought and gave us respite from the heat were welcome. But because they were truly 'scattered', none came my way; it just didn't seem fair. Not only did I envy my neighbour, who wouldn't have to water his lawn this week; I was also disappointed and a bit resentful. Didn't I deserve rain, too?

Actually, though, I have no right to be jealous of what others receive. So what if my neighbour gets rain and I don't? Or what if my colleague gets a promotion I felt should have been mine? What does it matter if a relative drives a nicer car or lives in a bigger house? None of us 'deserves' any of the good things that come our way. God gives to us out of love, not justice. If that were not so, none of us would have anything.

So I'll try even harder to be grateful for all the good that comes to me, regardless of what my neighbour receives. What God gives is the product of unmerited favour, neither earned nor deserved. That's God's amazing grace.

Prayer: *Father, help us to be grateful for what we have. May we never resent what comes to others. Amen*

Thought for the day: We all receive from God more than we deserve.

Richard L. Mabry (Texas, US)

Not Judging

Read Luke 14:7–14

Jesus said, 'Come to me, all you who are weary and burdened, and I will give you rest.'
Matthew 11:28 (NIV)

One morning when weeding my garden, I found among the flowers an orchid plant that once had been beautiful and exuberant. Now it was ugly and withered. With disdain, I pulled it out and threw it into the middle of the garden. Later, while watering the garden, I came across the most beautiful orchid I had ever seen. To my surprise, it was growing from the little plant I had thrown away.

This event brought to my memory the Bible story about the barren fig tree and the patient gardener (Luke 13:6–9). I compared my experience with the orchid to this. The patient gardener in that story is a good example for us. Instead of rejecting those who are downtrodden and burdened, such as prostitutes, homeless people, abandoned children and others society has forgotten, we can realise that all have gifts and talents.

We can welcome those who live on the margins of our cities and towns. When we do, we live in the spirit of Jesus Christ, who said, 'I did not come to judge the world, but to save it' (John 12:47).

Prayer: *Thank you, God, for all your blessings. Give us the desire and the courage to welcome those whom society has rejected. In Jesus' name. Amen*

Thought for the day: 'Do not judge, so you will not be judged' (see Matthew 7:1).

Miriam Marchini de Freitas (Sao Paulo, Brazil)

PRAYER FOCUS: ABANDONED CHILDREN

Ageing Gracefully

Read Psalm 90:1–17

My child, do not forget my teaching, but let your heart keep my commandments; for length of days and years of life and abundant welfare they will give you.

Proverbs 3:1–2 (NRSV)

As I have moved toward the end of my eighth decade, I have given more attention and thought to the issues that face those of us who are called senior citizens. Now, due to better nutrition and health care, more of us live beyond the biblical 'threescore years and ten' (Psalm 90:10, KJV).

In the community where I live, we recently celebrated the one-hundredth birthdays of three of our residents. Most people who live long lives seem to do so because they have regularly done what keeps the mind, body and spirit active, involved and useful.

Deuteronomy 4:40 promises long life if we keep God's commandments. Jesus called us 'the salt of the earth' and 'the light of the world' and told us to let our 'light shine before others' (Matthew 5:13–16). The secret of a meaningful Christian life, whether we live long or die young, is investing our years, our talents and our resources in doing for others what God, in love, has done for us. We age well, by God's grace, as we allow the redeeming love of Christ to shape us and flow through us to others.

Prayer: *We give thanks, O God, for the life that is the gift of your grace. Amen*

Thought for the day: For a rewarding life, invest yourself in serving God.

Elmer A. Dickson (Florida, US)

Small Group Questions

Wednesday 2 May

1. How would you respond if a young child turned up near your home as Heath did at Muriel's? How do you suppose the family reacted when Muriel brought Heath home?

2. Almost all families have a child-getting-lost story. What's yours? Why does the story get retold?

3. How has the phenomenon of missing children touched your community? What can and should the church do about it?

4. What 'ants' have led you into strange places in your spiritual journey? What did you learn from your travels? Who or what helped you to find your way back?

5. Heath wandered because of his love for something. How can our loves lead us away from God? How can we protect ourselves from loving the wrong things?

6. How can positive involvements in our lives interfere with our responsiveness to God? How can and should we limit good activities? How can good activities in the church become hindrances to growing in our faith?

7. Where do you find yourself being tempted over and over again? How can you prepare yourself spiritually for the next time you face this? Do you want the group members to offer advice and suggestions?

Wednesday 9 May

1. Who was your first crush, and how old were you? When and where did you first fall seriously in love? What was the outcome of that love?

2. Do you know anyone like this woman, someone who has dreamed of love and prayed for a mate but did not find one? What can the church offer such people? How do we sometimes make their situations more painful for them?

3. What contributes to making people feel bad about their limitations or imperfections? How can and should the church respond differently to people with disabilities from the way those outside the church do?

4. Do you think everyone feels somewhat as Lautan does, flawed and judged for it? Why do you say this?

5. What does your church do to welcome people with disabilities? How could your building(s) and activities be more accessible to them? What can you do to become more welcoming?

6. What good thing(s) have you prayed for but not received? How has this affected your ideas about God and his will? How can we protect ourselves from becoming bitter or angry with God when our prayers for good things are not answered?

7. What have you prayed about for a long time? What helps you to keep praying and believing when you see no results?

Wednesday 16 May

1. What current political or news slogan reflects on you or troubles you, and why? If you think you don't care about political labels, think about how you would feel if someone called you by a label that doesn't fit your position. Are you sure you don't care?

2. What situation did you think of when you first read this meditation? How did its message compare to your response and feelings about the situation? Were you challenged by Richard's words or affirmed by them? Why?

3. Is it acceptable to judge people's faith by their political positions? Why or why not? How can Christians model love in spite of political differences?

4. Read aloud James 3:6–10. How do we 'curse' people without using literal curses? What situations tempt you to use harsh words?

5. When have someone's words been a 'blessing' to you recently? Why do you say this? When have you blessed someone with your words?

6. What is your definition of hospitality? How does hospitality extend beyond food and drink to attitudes and words?

7. Who has helped you to come to know yourself as dearly loved and valued by God? What did that person or those persons do that led you to this?

Wednesday 23 May

1. Do you think it is possible to live in such a way that we have no regrets? What makes you say this? Do you know anyone who has come close to living that kind of life?

2. How can we let go of regrets? How does holding on to them limit us?

3. Looking back on your life, what would you most like to change? Is wishing for that the same thing as having regrets?

4. What is the best decision you have made in your life? Do you identify it as such because of your feelings about it or because of its result(s)?

5. What have you learned from your bad decisions? How can our bad decisions help us to become clearer about what really matters?

6. Read aloud 2 Corinthians 7:9–10. What does it say about regret and repentance? In light of this passage, what would you say is the difference between shame and repentance?

7. Does admitting a sin make you feel better or worse? According to the Corinthians passage you just heard, how should it feel and what should be the result of repentance?

8. What does being cleansed and forgiven feel like to you? Have you always thought of forgiveness in this way?

Wednesday 30 May

1. What sayings that you heard in childhood from adults still echo in your mind? In what situations does each of them come to mind? Does remembering them affect your actions? If so, in what way(s)? If not, how did you 'turn them off'?

2. Can you picture your parents dealing with you as Woody's father did him? How did those who brought you up usually deal with your wrongdoings? What trait would you have most hoped for in your childhood adult contacts?

3. What childhood prank or misdeed do you remember clearly? Did you get away with it or get caught? Whichever is true, do you think that's why you remember it?

4. What is your first memory of feeling guilt? How old were you at the time, and what caused you to feel guilty? Do you still feel guilty?

5. What physical symptoms do you feel when your heart and/or conscience are troubled? What gives you relief at these times?

6. How does forgiveness feel? What physical sensation would you compare it to, and why?

7. What teaching from your childhood or teenage years still offers you direction?

Wednesday 6 June

1. When has an encounter with a poor person taught you something about God or led to an insight about faith? What did you learn or realise?

2. What does God want us to do to help poor people and neglected children? How is your church reaching out to these groups? Where would you like it to be doing more?

3. Read aloud James 2:1–9. How many friends do you have who come from very different social settings or cultures from yours? In the light of the passage from James, does your answer cause you to feel uncomfortable, proud of yourself or something else, and why?

4. Are most of the people in your church pretty much like you, or is your congregation diverse in race, social class, languages and so on? How are unusual people treated when they visit, if they do? Have any of them returned or stayed to become part of your community of faith?

5. Are some concerns too small to pray about? Why do you say this? What is the smallest concern you've prayed about? Was that prayer answered?

6. Who taught you to appreciate some special kind of beauty? How did this come about, and what was the beauty you came to see? How does the absence of beauty affect life? How does appreciating beauty affect life?

7. What questions do today's scripture verse raise for you? Do you think Jesus actually meant that all our prayers will be answered if we believe hard enough? If not, what do you think he meant?

Wednesday 13 June

1. If you could choose one famous person, living or dead (besides Jesus), from any country or era, to meet, whom would you choose, and why?

2. What languages have you studied and do you speak? What is the value of learning more than one language?

3. How much time and thought do you give to preparing yourself for a time of prayer? Do you have a personal 'ritual' you go through as you prepare for your devotional time? What is or might be the value of having one?

4. Do you use a different vocabulary when you pray from the one you use in ordinary conversation? Why or why not?

5. How can we balance reverence for God with intimacy when we pray? In the way we live day by day?

6. Tyler speaks of God as regal, having a throne. What images of or ideas about God might make it hard for us to approach God in prayer?

7. What is your favourite way of addressing God when you pray, and why? Where and when did you come to think of God this way?

Wednesday 20 June

1. What do you find attractive about small churches? How does being small limit a church? What do you find attractive about large churches? How does being large limit a church?

2. What is your first memory of being in church? Who was with you or took you? What emotions do you associate with this memory, and why?

3. How have changes in the economy affected the way you relate to and serve in your church? What does your church do to help those affected by economic hardship? Where do you wish it were doing more?

4. What can a church that has little material wealth offer its community?

5. How do you respond to the statement, 'We learned that even when our pockets are empty, God's love keeps us rich in our hearts'? Have you ever experienced feeling like that—rich in your heart even though you had no money? What makes or would make that feeling possible?

6. What is your definition of generosity? Whom do you picture as living generously, and why?

7. What non-material gifts has God given you that you might share with others? How could you go about sharing them as a ministry in your neighbourhood?

Wednesday 27 June

1. Does the opening sentence of this meditation make you feel guilty, inspire you or affect you in some other way? Why?

2. What Bible reading plans have you used in the past? Why did you either stick with them or give up on them? What plan or routine guides your Bible reading now?

3. Which prophet or other Old Testament character is your favourite, and why? Which Old Testament story did you first learn, where, and when?

4. What are some verses, stories or commands from the Bible that trouble or puzzle you? How have you tried to make sense of them in relation to your life? How have you made progress in understanding and applying them?

5. What does the saying 'the devil is in the details' mean to you? Give an example from your life that might illustrate it.

6. Do you think God is concerned about every tiny detail of our lives—whether we find a parking space, what clothes we wear on any given day, where we go every day, and so on? Why do you say yes or no? If the opposite of your answer were true, how might it change the way you live?

7. Matthew 10:30 says that God knows even the number of hairs on our head. Why do you think that verse is in the Bible? How does it apply to your life? What little things do you need God's help with this week?

Wednesday 4 July

1. Did your ancestors emigrate from another country? If you don't have a clear sense of this, what would you like to know more about, and why?

2. What or who has given you the courage to dream about a better life? What part did/does your relationship with God play in your dreams for a better future for yourself? For others?

3. Do you believe God wants a better future for everyone? If so, what part do you play in that better future? What part can your faith community play in the better future God offers those near you? For those far away?

4. How does your church respond to immigrants and other newcomers to your community? What do you do to draw them into your fellowship? If you do nothing, why so?

5. Read Micah 6:8 aloud. Do you see any tension between 'doing justice' and 'loving kindness'? If so, how do you reconcile those two calls from the prophet Micah? If not, where do you see them being lived out simultaneously?

6. When was your last opportunity to show kindness and mercy? Did you? If not, why not? If so, how?

Wednesday 11 July

1. What is your favourite mental image or memory of people holding hands? Why do you like it? What does the image say to you?

2. Are you more a 'toucher'—touching others and welcoming them to touch you—or more a 'hands-off' person in your interactions? What makes you the kind of person you are? How do you deal with those unlike you?

3. When was the last time another believer held your hand, either literally or figuratively? What did that interaction mean to you? How do you experience God being present in such situations?

4. How do you sense God 'holding' you? In what settings are you aware of God's comforting presence? If you do not sense God's presence, what do you think when others talk about that?

5. Read Mark 8:22–26 and Mark 10:46–52. Why do you suppose Jesus touched one blind man but not the other in these stories? What do the two stories say to you about how to deal with people?

6. Who has taught you about 'faithful and steadfast love'? How and in what relationships have you expressed God's steadfast love in the last week? Month? Where do you want to do better in that?

Wednesday 18 July

1. Who is/was your favourite relative, and why? How can even favourite people get on our nerves? In such times, what can we do to help change our perspective?

2. Do you agree that what we expect shapes what we get in relationships? Either way you answer, give a personal example to support your opinion.

3. How does God want us to deal with people we find difficult? Have you ever been able to change your opinion about, and response to, such a person? If so, how?

4. Who finds you difficult, and what do you do that bothers him/her/them? Are you working on changing that behaviour? Do you think God wants you to?

5. Besides Proverbs 11:27, what are some other Bible verses or stories that reinforce the idea that what we look for influences what we see?

6. In whom have you seen unexpected goodness? What can God say to us through such experiences? What has God said to you through one of them?

Wednesday 25 July

1. How would you feel if you had been in the restaurant with Jonathan during the experience he recounts here? Do you think details such as how we behave in restaurants matter to God? Why or why not?

2. What's on the 'menu' of what you most often ask God to do? Who are the people you mention most often to God?

3. 'We restrict our prayer life when we ask God for answers so specific that we close our eyes to some other response.' How is that statement true? How is it not true?

4. Read aloud Ephesians 3:20. When has God surprised you and gone beyond what you asked or even thought of? Do you think God does this often?

5. How might reading today's meditation change the way you pray?

6. What's the latest new pattern or practice you've tried in your praying? Why did you try it? What did you get out of it? Will you keep doing it or incorporate some part of it into your way of praying? Why or why not?

Wednesday 1 August

1. What was your first response when you began reading this meditation and came to the word 'Communist'? What associations came to mind?

2. What does the fading of Communism over the last few decades say to you about what God is doing in the world and how God does it? About our fears of those who are different from us?

3. If you were part of the Church when you were a teenager and young adult, how did you present that part of your life to your friends? If you were not part of the Church, how did you feel about and talk about people who were?

4. On a scale of 1 (reluctant) to 10 (very proud) how would you rate your feelings about being part of your church? On a similar scale regarding being publicly Christian, where would you place yourself, and why? Why might your two responses be different?

5. Have you ever experienced resistance or persecution for being Christian? If so, when and how? How common is such treatment in your culture?

6. What would it look like for you to live your daily life 'to the fullest, in God's will and for his glory'? How would your life be different from what it is now? What keeps you from doing this?

Wednesday 8 August

1. What forgotten courtesy or social practice from years ago do you wish were still in fashion today, and why?

2. If you were writing a thank-you note to God for something that happened or came to you this week, what would it be? Why are you thankful?

3. When was the last time you wrote a thank-you note, to whom and about what? Who taught you to write thank-you notes or to say thank you? Why are these practices important?

4. Where do good manners and behaving in a Christian way overlap? What is the difference between the two?

5. Do you, like June, expect to be thanked for the gifts you give? Should we give only to those who express thanks or should we keep giving regardless of response? Why do you say this?

6. Have you ever kept a gratitude journal, listing what you were grateful for? What might be the value of doing this? What four things would go on your gratitude list today? How can being grateful affect our outlook on life?

7. Read aloud 1 Thessalonians 5:17–18. What in these verses challenges you? What is the difference between giving thanks *in* all things and giving thanks *for* all things? Why is the difference important?

Wednesday 15 August

1. When have you been called on to do something in a job or within your community of faith that was a stretch for you? How did the situation turn out? What if anything did you learn in the process?

2. What's your favourite part of the Mary and Martha story? What words or actions recounted in it touch you most, and why?

3. Who in your congregation is quick to respond to members in time of loss? What does your congregation do to help grieving parishioners? Where do you wish your congregation did more?

4. Who's the most accomplished worrier you know? Give a picture of what qualifies the person for this title.

5. Is worry ever necessary? Why do you say this? What is the connection, if any, between worry and faith (or trusting God)?

6. Are you more like Mary—a mystic—or more like Martha—a doer—in your faith? What do you like about the kind of believer you are?

7. How do you relate to Michelle's statements about the Holy Spirit? How are you aware of the Holy Spirit acting in your life of faith?

Wednesday 22 August

1. Who is a good enough friend to you to challenge you when you behave badly? When was the last time this happened? How did you respond?

2. When do we have the right and responsibility to speak to other believers about their behaviour? If you think we never should, why do you think this?

3. Today's scripture reading says that when we serve the hungry, imprisoned, sick or poor, we serve Christ. When did you last encounter Christ in one of these people? Do you meet Christ in this way often enough? Too much?

4. Besides today's scripture reading, what other Bible passages challenge you regarding how you respond to needy and homeless people?

5. How does your congregation reach out to needy people? Which group mentioned in today's reading do you do the best job of serving, and how do you serve them? Which group do you serve least well?

6. Do you agree with Steven's assessment that he sinned in responding as he did to the window washer? Why or why not? Was he too hard on himself?

Wednesday 29 August

1. When or by what are you tempted to jealousy? In what situations do you find yourself thinking 'I wish I had ________' or 'I wish God would give me ________'?

2. Read Matthew 5:43–45. Is the opposite of this passage also true, that God sends bad weather on both the just and unjust? How would you respond to someone who says that harsh weather is God's punishment?

3. How do you respond when news reports after disasters feature some people saying 'God protected us' when others died or lost everything? In dangerous situations, does God favour some believers but not others and some unbelievers but not others?

4. Are opportunities like access to education or being born in a wealthy country 'blessings' intentionally given by God to some but withheld from others? Why do you say this? If such opportunities are not specifically given to selected individuals by God, should we still express thanks for them?

5. Do you agree that we don't 'deserve' any of the good that comes to us? Why or why not?

6. Would you prefer that God be just or that God be merciful? Why?

Journal page

Journal page

Journal page

Embracing Dusty Detours

A spiritual search for depth in desert places

Lynne E. Chandler

'*I feel at last that I am embracing the present moment of life. I haven't arrived, I'm just resting; resting beside quiet waters that inevitably churn and stir from time to time and turn into strong currents that drag me back into the river of the hectic everyday.*'

This book takes you on a quest through the bustling chaos of Middle Eastern city life and the drama of a youth-led revolution to endless stretches of rolling desert sand, and Bible places from the top of Mount Sinai to the shores of Galilee. This quest, along life's dusty detours, is in search of oases of all kinds—people, places, and little glimpses of eternity.

As in *Embracing a Concrete Desert*, Lynne Chandler relates her experiences in a compelling mixture of laughter, tears and raw honesty, using lyrical prose and poems. The journey is often one lurch forward and two steps backward, and rarely in a straight line, but she shares how it has led her to deeper insights into faith and greater reliance on God than she ever imagined.

ISBN 978 1 84101 829 4 £6.99
To order a copy of this book, please turn to the order form on page 159.

Jesus, Name above all Names

32 Bible studies on the person and work of Jesus

Anne Le Tissier

This book offers straightforward, devotionally based Bible study material on 32 names and titles ascribed to Jesus in scripture. From 'Advocate' to 'Word of God', the studies consider what we can learn about who Jesus is and what he has done for us from these different names and titles. The material includes extended reflection on the theme, questions for response, prayers and suggestions for further Bible reading.

Prepared from articles originally published in *Woman Alive* magazine, *Jesus: Name above all Names* is ideal for small group use or individual Quiet Day or retreat reading.

ISBN 978 0 85746 085 1 £8.99
To order a copy of this book, please turn to the order form on page 159.

Dreaming of Home

Homecoming as a model for renewal and mission

Michael Mitton

Finding a sense of 'home', a special place of acceptance and belonging, is a fundamental human longing. In this powerful and profound book, Michael Mitton shows how it is, in fact, an essential part of both personal development and spiritual renewal. Drawing on his own experience of the 'homecoming' journey, he considers how we can go about finding our true home within God's eternal kingdom, how to identify the forces within us that may hinder this search, and the importance of churches offering a welcoming home to all.

Each chapter concludes with questions for personal reflection or group discussion and the book also features an imaginative retelling of the parable of the prodigal son, addressing some of the issues raised through a story-based approach.

ISBN 978 1 84101 877 5 £7.99
To order a copy of this book, please turn to the order form on page 159.

God's Church; My Place

What it means to belong to a Christian community

Steve Tilley

What does being involved in church mean in practical terms?

Christian communities are full of people exercising ministries, doing useful work and, well, helping others. How do we find our place? *God's Church; My Place* is a book for people who want to serve God and need to work out the where, when and how. It covers important topics such as church structure, worship, prayers, serving and the precarious state of the coffee—and all thoroughly biblically. It will not push you into leadership but will value your membership.

Like Steve's previous book, *Mustard Seed Shavings*, each chapter ends with a pause for thought, a couple of discussion questions and a brief prayer. It might be useful to read the book with a small group.

ISBN 978 0 85746 011 0 £6.99
To order a copy of this book, please turn to the order form on page 159.

Encircling the Christian Year

Liturgies and reflections for the seasons of the Church

Barbara Mosse

The seasons of the Church's year parallel those of the natural world, gifting us with opportunities for spiritual life and growth. The watchfulness of Advent with its symbolism of light and darkness gives way to the explosion of joy as we welcome the birth of Christ; the sombre season of Lent leads us through the despair of the cross to the wonder and joy of Easter. But our journey into God is far more than a succession of spiritual high points, and perhaps the weeks of 'Ordinary Time' encourage us to persist in our walk with Christ during those times when nothing much seems to be happening.

Beginning with Advent Sunday, *Encircling the Christian Year* presents a series of short liturgies for each week of the Church calendar, including a Bible reading, reflection and prayers, suitable for both individual and small group use. Special liturgies are also provided for the major festivals and 'red letter days', celebrating the saints and events most closely connected with the life of Christ. As well as engaging with the liturgical seasons, the book invites us to deeper prayer; to grow in our relationship with the God who loves us and accompanies us through all the seasons of our lives.

ISBN 978 0 85746 045 5 £8.99
To order a copy of this book, please turn to the order form on page 159.

Bible Reading Resources Pack

Thank you for reading BRF Bible reading notes. BRF has been producing a variety of Bible reading notes for over 90 years, helping people all over the UK and the world connect with the Bible on a personal level every day.

Could you help us find other people who would enjoy our notes?

We produce a Bible Reading Resource Pack for church groups to use to encourage regular Bible reading.

This **FREE** pack contains:

- Samples of all BRF Bible reading notes.
- Our Resources for Personal Bible Reading catalogue, providing all you need to know about our Bible reading notes.
- A ready-to-use church magazine feature about BRF notes.
- Ready-made sermon and all-age service ideas to help your church into the Bible (ideal for Bible Sunday events).
- And much more!

How to order your FREE pack:

- Visit: www.biblereadingnotes.org.uk/request-a-bible-reading-resources-pack/
- Telephone: 01865 319700
- Post: Complete the form below and post to: Bible Reading Resource Pack, BRF, 15 The Chambers, Vineyard, Abingdon, OX14 3FE

Name..

Address ....

.... Postcode.......................................

Telephone ....

Email..

Please send me.................................Bible Reading Resources Pack(s).

This pack is produced free of charge for all UK addresses but, if you wish to offer a donation towards our costs, this would be appreciated. If you require a pack to be sent outside of the UK, please contact us for details of postage and packing charges. Tel: +44 1865 319700. Thank you.

BRF is a Registered Charity

Subscriptions

The Upper Room is published in January, May and September.

Individual subscriptions

The subscription rate for orders for 4 or fewer copies includes postage and packing: THE UPPER ROOM annual individual subscription £14.10

Church subscriptions

Orders for 5 copies or more, sent to ONE address, are post free:
THE UPPER ROOM annual church subscription £11.10

Please do not send payment with order for a church subscription. We will send an invoice with your first order.

Please note that the annual billing period for church subscriptions runs from 1 May to 30 April.

Copies of the notes may also be obtained from Christian bookshops.

Single copies of *The Upper Room* will cost £3.70. Prices valid until 30 April 2013.

Individual Subscriptions

☐ I would like to take out a subscription myself (complete your name and address details only once)

☐ I would like to give a gift subscription (please complete both name and address sections below)

Your name ....

Your address ....

.... Postcode.......................................

Your telephone number...

Gift subscription name...

Gift subscription address...

.... Postcode.......................................

Gift message (20 words max)...

....

Please send *The Upper Room* beginning with the September 2012 / January 2013 / May 2013 issue: (delete as applicable)

THE UPPER ROOM ☐ £14.10

Please complete the payment details below and send, with appropriate payment, to: BRF, 15 The Chambers, Vineyard, Abingdon OX14 3FE

Total enclosed £.......... (cheques should be made payable to 'BRF')

Payment by ☐ cheque ☐ postal order ☐ Visa ☐ Mastercard ☐ Switch

Card no: ☐☐☐☐☐☐☐☐☐☐☐☐☐☐☐☐☐☐☐

Expires: ☐☐☐☐ Security code: ☐☐☐

Issue no (Switch): ☐☐☐☐

Signature (essential if paying by credit/Switch card) ....

☐ Please do not send me further information about BRF publications

☐ Please send me a Bible reading resources pack to encourage Bible reading in my church

BRF is a Registered Charity

Church Subscriptions

☐ Please send me ...... copies of *The Upper Room* September 2012 / January 2013 / May 2013 issue (delete as applicable)

Name..

Address ....

.... Postcode.......................................

Telephone ....

Email..

Please send this completed form to:
BRF, 15 The Chambers, Vineyard, Abingdon OX14 3FE

Please do not send payment with this order. We will send an invoice with your first order.

Christian bookshops: All good Christian bookshops stock BRF publications. For your nearest stockist, please contact BRF.

Telephone: The BRF office is open between 09.15 and 17.30. To place your order, telephone 01865 319700; fax 01865 319701.

Web: Visit www.brf.org.uk

☐ Please send me a Bible reading resources pack to encourage Bible reading in my church

BRF is a Registered Charity

ORDERFORM

REF	TITLE	PRICE	QTY	TOTAL
829 4	Embracing Dusty Detours	£6.99		
085 1	Jesus, Name above all Names	£8.99		
877 5	Dreaming of Home	£7.99		
011 0	God's Church; My Place	£6.99		
045 5	Encircling the Christian Year	£8.99		
		Postage and packing		
		Donation		
		TOTAL		

POSTAGE AND PACKING CHARGES				
Order value	UK	Europe	Surface	Air Mail
£7.00 & under	£1.25	£3.00	£3.50	£5.50
£7.01–£30.00	£2.25	£5.50	£6.50	£10.00
Over £30.00	FREE	prices on request		

Name ______________________ Account Number ____________

Address ____

______________________ Postcode ____________

Telephone Number______________________

Email ____

Payment by: ❑ Cheque ❑ Mastercard ❑ Visa ❑ Postal Order ❑ Maestro

Card no ☐☐☐☐ ☐☐☐☐ ☐☐☐☐ ☐☐☐☐ ☐☐☐

Valid from ☐☐☐☐ Expires ☐☐☐☐ Issue no. ☐☐☐

Security code* ☐☐☐ *Last 3 digits on the reverse of the card. ESSENTIAL IN ORDER TO PROCESS YOUR ORDER

Shaded boxes for Maestro use only

Signature ______________________ Date ____________

All orders must be accompanied by the appropriate payment.

Please send your completed order form to:

BRF, 15 The Chambers, Vineyard, Abingdon OX14 3FE
Tel. 01865 319700 / Fax. 01865 319701 Email: enquiries@brf.org.uk

❑ Please send me further information about BRF publications.

Available from your local Christian bookshop.

BRF is a Registered Charity